Life After Life

bj King

Life After Life

bj King

Copyright © 2025 by bj King

Published by 1st World Publishing
P.O. Box 2211, Fairfield, Iowa 52556
tel: 641-209-5000 • fax: 866-440-5234
web: www.1stworldpublishing.com

First Edition

ISBN Softcover: 9781421835884

LCCN: Library of Congress Cataloging-in-Publication Data

All rights reserved. No part of this book may be reproduced or utilized in any form or by any means, electronic or mechanical, including photocopying or recording, or by any information storage and retrieval system, without permission in writing from the author.

This material has been written and published for educational purposes to enhance one's well-being. In regard to health issues, the information is not intended as a substitute for appropriate care and advice from health professionals, nor does it equate to the assumption of medical or any other form of liability on the part of the publisher or author. The publisher and author shall have neither liability nor responsibility to any person or entity with respect to loss, damages, or injury claimed to be caused directly or indirectly by any information in this book.

Dedicated to Edward who is gone from
me now physically, but was there when I needed him
and is here now when I need someone to talk to.

My eternal gratitude to Bill Browning who
Edward sent into life to rescue me financially
after he left me.

Gratitude to Mary Bosse, Judi Rider, Larry McCaslin, Sheri Hartman
and Kelley Kay King who edited the books

Table of Contents

1. bj's Story and the Beginning of Channeling 7
2. Communication with Mother 25
3. Communication with John 29
4. Death: Life's Greatest Adventure 31
5. Dimensions 40
6. First Communication with Edward 46
7. Different Versions of the Afterlife 47
8. Comments from Edward in the Afterlife 49
9. Edward's Experiences in Summerland 61
10. Edward's Comments on Religion and Prayer 72
11. Comments from Edward in the Afterlife 81
12. Edward On Love and Marriage 93
13. Comments from Edward on Spiritual Gifts 105
14. Consciously Facing Life, Death and Dying 111
15. The Bordo and Levels of Life between Lives 119
16. Judgment 128
17. Borderland, Midland, Highland 133
18. Hell and the Law of Retribution 143
19. Methods of Contacting the Spiritual World 150

1.

bj's Story and the Beginning of Channeling

In 1979 I was what I thought of as a middle-class American housewife living in Lubbock, Texas. I was married and had two children: a boy, 6 and a girl, 11. I was a member of an Episcopal Church, president of the women of the church, secretary of the diocese and Camp Fire leader for my daughter's troop. I appeared to be happily married. My husband was a firefighter and had an automotive garage where he worked on his days off from the fire department. He worked approximate 100 hours a week.

My parents lived near me and I checked on my Mother daily and went by to do her hair twice a week. My father and I have never been close. I called my Dad when I took her to the hospital. My father believed she was having an allergic reaction to something and did not respond to my call for help. During the next week, she had two heart attacks and died on March 9, 1979.

The day of my Mother's funeral, my father insisted that my sister-in-law and I clear out my mother's personal belongings. His sisters were in town for the funeral and he wanted them to have my Mother's clothes. When we reached the bottom of her lingerie drawer there was a long-stemmed red rose that I had sent her years before on my birthday. The rose, the vase and the card were wrapped in a great deal of aluminum foil to protect them and a card was attached to the outside in her handwriting that read, "Receiving this rose fulfilled a lifetime fantasy."

The evening of the day of the funeral, my husband expected me to go out to eat with his family who came to the funeral from Abilene, Texas. He told me to drive his three sisters-in-law to our home and entertain them while he took his brothers to his shop to show them some new equipment. His lack of compassion for my loss and this act of betrayal of my feelings of grief and loss caused a severe break in my feelings toward him and my commitment to the marriage.

Within eight weeks, my father brought home a woman from a bar and moved her into what I considered to be my Mother's home. He called and told me she had had her children by Cesarean section as I had and that having sex with her was as good as he imagined it would be to have sex with me.

The same day of my mother's death, the priest of our parish and his wife moved to Oklahoma City, OK. He and I and his wife had been close friends. When they heard of my mother's death they offered to return to Lubbock, but I could not accept their inconveniencing themselves for me in that way when they were in the middle of a move.

The next week I received a letter from Edward, the priest of our parish. He and I had worked closely together at the church for three years in a professional capacity. His letter was meant to support me spiritually to deal with my mother's death. I was so deep in grief and so distraught by my husband's insensitivity it took me a while to respond. When I did respond he began to write to me on a regular basis. We exchanged letters over a period of six months and realized gradually that we were in love with each other. He got a divorce shortly after arriving in Oklahoma City and went back into geology, which is what he did before becoming a priest. He continued to work as an unpaid priest to substitute when other priests were on vacation.

In his letters he invited me and my children to move to Oklahoma City to be with him and that he would take care of us and support me to go to college, something I had always wanted to do, but could not afford.

When my husband discovered that I was considering leaving him, he was panicked and attempted to get three psychologists to agree that I was mentally unstable so he could have me temporarily committed to a hospital while he tried to convince me to stay with him. I did not know that the law in Texas allowed a husband this power over a wife. When we visited the psychologists, I thought we were interviewing them to find one we felt comfortable with as a marriage counselor. Only when the third one turned to my husband and said, "Mr. King, I think she is the sanest person to ever walk through my door" did I realize I was in a sanity hearing. This only reinforced my desire to flee my marriage.

In November of 1979 Edward invited me and my children again to move to Oklahoma City to be with him. I divorced my husband the children and

I moved to Oklahoma on November 9, 1979, exactly eight months after my Mother's death. Edward and I were to be married in two weeks. On the fourth night of our being together he died of a heart attack in my bed after we had made love.

The next day I received a call from the Bishop of Oklahoma who notified me I would not be welcome at the funeral, and if I attended I would be asked to leave. He also stated that I was excommunicated from taking communion in the Episcopal Church. I received the same message from the Bishop of West Texas. I was devastated. Only much later did I realize this was God's way of getting me to go directly to God without an intermediary.

The next day my ex-husband came to Oklahoma City and took the children back to Texas to live with him. He attempted to get me to agree to return to him and our life together. I had not taken much money from the marriage knowing that Edward was going to take care of the children and myself. I was not in a financial or emotional position to keep the children with me. I felt they would be better off returning to the home, school and friends they knew while I figured out what to do next.

For days I sat and looked out the window of our condo and tried to figure out, "Who am I?" I tried to write, to clear my mind, to make my mind have sequential thoughts. I tried to examine "Who am I?" on paper and in my heart. If I was no longer my mother's daughter, because she was dead, who was I? If my father did not want or need to relate to me, because he had a new family, who was I? If my friends had abandoned me, I had no job, no position in the community or church and then who was I? If I was not John's wife, because I chose to leave, and I was not there to mother my children, then, who was I? If I was not Edward's lover, because he was dead, who was I? Was I anyone other than the roles I played for other people? Was this black void the answer to not playing roles? I sat in a rocking chair with a pencil and paper on my lap and wrote: "I AM...? I AM....? I AM...? I AM...? I AM...? I AM . . .?" I was unable to come up with a description of what was left when all the roles were removed. I did not at all understand the message of what I was saying to myself on the paper, or the enormity of the message coming from my soul: "When all else is stripped away, the I AM, which equals God Presence, remains. Before and after all else, we are God playing roles as Humans."

After a few weeks I had to go to work and all I knew how to do was to be a bank teller. I quickly realized I could not support myself on a bank teller's salary. I had read one book on self-actualization which suggested, "Fake it 'til you make it." So I charged three banker suits and began to see myself as management. Within a very short time I was promoted to assistant head teller and soon after that was invited by the University of Oklahoma to teach bank teller security all over the state. They never asked if I had a degree or credentials to teach.

This was God's way of getting me used to talking in front of groups of people to talk about something I already knew so I would lose my fear public speaking, since later I would later be expected to talk to groups about metaphysical subjects.

I was then offered an even higher position with a Savings and Loan Association as a bank consultant to create a teller training program for their tellers. This was during the time period when Savings and Loans were becoming banks. Our verbal agreement was that they would hire me as a consultant and then when I created the program they would hire me as an employee to train all the tellers in all 28 of their branches. The day I gave them the program, they let me go thanking me for my work and letting me know that one of their officers could now do the training.

Three years after my mom's and Edward's death I was again devastated. As Divine timing would have it, a man I had been seeing periodically, when he traveled through Oklahoma, called from California and invited me to fly to California to go on a ten day sailing trip with him on his 35 foot sail boat. I had never been sailing, and feeling lost and without direction, I agreed to go. When I arrived in August 1982, and because (the air-conditioning in the plane had quit working.) I was exhausted and soaking wet from perspiration.

I was taken to a dive shop where I was to be fitted with a wet suit and diving equipment. The suit was still damp from the previous user and my body was damp and clammy from sweating in the airplane. The suit was built for a fourteen year old boy with no ass, which obviously was not my body dimension. I struggled into it partially and waddled out into the showroom with the suit hanging down in my crotch at least 12 inches. My intention was to show the owner that the suit didn't fit. He was oriental and spoke maybe the only English word he knew, "Perfect." There was no way in hell it was perfect, but I didn't have the strength to argue.

I was not naïve enough to think there wasn't going to be sex involved in my visit, but I did expect to get to take a shower and a nap first. That did not happen. My host had me across the bed as soon as we entered his home. Laying there watching the clock numbers flipping registered his six minute recovery time I was scared, angry and feeling helpless and hopeless. I didn't know it was humanly possible for a man to recover an erection so quickly.

I immediately regretted taking him up on his offer of a "free" vacation. He was Jewish and had survived a German prison camp and I wondered if that was what caused him to be so driven to have sex so repetitiously.

The next day aboard the boat I became seasick. My host had assured me he could sail the boat by himself. He yelled at me all day, "Move this, do this, duck!" I was so sick, angry and hurt I could not even speak. He then anchored and cooked Hungarian goulash. After ten days of being verbally and sexually attacked and sea sick I put on the wet suit, the skin diving gear, all but putting the air intake in my mouth, and jumped into the Pacific to kill myself. I figured I didn't have to worry about going to hell, I was already there. I knew for sure I had truly pissed God off. A Yacht had anchored beside us during the night and the men on deck noticed that the right kinds of air bubbles were not coming up around where I had jumped in. One of the men jumped in and rescued me.

When I finally got back to Oklahoma City I noticed a book on my coffee table that I had bought in Texas to read aloud to Edward in the moving van on the way to Oklahoma. The name of the book is *Illusions* by Richard Bach. On the back cover of the book it says, "Here is a test to find whether your mission on Earth is finished. If you're alive, it isn't."

I broke down and started to laugh and cry at the same time and said to God, "If you've got a mission for me in this life you need to tell me. I'll go anywhere, do anything, and say anything you want if you will just talk to me." No big booming Charleston Heston kind-of-voice, which I had been expecting, said anything. Even though I had been a Christian since the age of six, and always involved in Church as an adult, I had never completely turned my life over to God for fear of having to go to Africa to be a missionary.

Since I neither heard nor felt any response from God, I went to a Walden's bookstore looking for a book on how to find your life purpose. Being a good Christian, albeit an ex-communicated one, I knew better than to go close to the occult section of the bookstore. That day I was so depressed I walked past the occult section. When I did, a book was thrown off the shelf in front of me. Astonished, I picked it up off the floor. The name of the book was *Psychic Energy* by Joseph Weed. The book was printed on newsprint and was not attractive. Being a Libra I don't do ugly and being afraid of anything psychic I put the book back on the shelf and went back to psychology, self-help and religion where I thought my help should come from. There was no book at that time on how to find one's life purpose. Even more depressed, I started back out of the bookstore. As I passed the same shelf where I had returned the *Psychic Energy* book

I noticed that the book now had a glowing white light moving around it. This really freaked me out. Things did not light up in my reality at that time. I am a very pragmatic person and I couldn't deny that something strange was happening so I bought the book.

On the way home I made a bargain with God that I would do what I used to do with the *Bible*: ask a question, close my eyes, open to a page, put my finger down, open my eyes and accept the message my finger landed on as a message from God in answer to my question. I did this as soon as I arrived home. The page I opened to, with my eyes closed, was a page describing a meditation to do to receive inspired writing from one's soul.

I accepted that this had to be a response from God since what I was asking for was direct contact with God or my soul to try to find out why I'm here. I was afraid to get this wrong so I did everything as it was described in the book. I took a shower to symbolically cleanse my aura even though I didn't know what an aura was. I took the phone off the hook so I wouldn't be disturbed and lit a white candle. I sat on the couch with my spine straight, wearing a loose fitting robe with my bare feet on the floor and pen and paper on my lap.

I began to breathe and count as was described in the book. I took a deep breath and counted internally, one, one, one, and exhaled. I took another deep breath and internally counted two, two, two, and exhaled. I took another deep breath and counted internally three, three, three, and exhaled. I began to internally count backward from ten to one. My left brain was going nuts saying, "This is the dumbest thing you've ever done. For God's sake put the phone on the hook and go get a job." I refused and thought, "No, I've tried all that and it didn't work. I'm going to sit here until God says something to me." I just continued to breathe and count as was directed. After a short time on the right side of my head there were words, not audible words, not a voice, just words like a separate thought form from the argument my left brain was still giving me. The words were, "Through this pen will come the words you need..." I waited thinking my hand was going to write by itself. The words repeated themselves several times before my impatience caused me to loudly say, "What?"

The reaction was like a record skipping a beat. There were five more words. I realized that I should write what was there. As I wrote there would be more words. Seven legal-sized pages later, the words stopped. I reread what had been written. Basically it was God or my soul asking me what I wanted to do now and where I wanted to be and it said that I would find that God's will for my life would very closely parallel my own heart's desire.

The message also suggested that I should try the meditation for 30 days before giving up and to write out my heart's desires.

Since there were now two streams of thought in my head I wondered if I had become schizophrenic. I had no one I could talk to about what was happening. All my friends had turned against me when I ran away with the priest and I knew no one else who meditated or expected to hear directly from God. When I first read what had been written I tried to believe I had made it up, but in the message it specifically said try this meditation for 30 days and I knew I would not tell myself to do anything for thirty days.

As directed in the writing, I wrote a list of what I desired to do:

I want to do something creative.

I want to work from home in case my children want to come to live with me.

I want to do something that helps people to communicate since this seemed to me to be the biggest problem in the World.

I want to do something I can't be fired from.

I want to teach adults something they really want to learn.

I want to help people to self-actualize. (I had read the one book about self-actualization and thought it would be great if everyone became all they were capable of being. Actually, I was trying to impress God, if this was in fact God that I was communicating with, that I knew such a big word.)

I went to bed and slept soundly. The next morning I once again questioned my sanity. How could I be sane and have two separate thought forms happening in my mind? Since the message indicated I should do the meditation for 30 days, I decided to try the meditation again. I did the same ritual of taking a shower, taking the phone off the hook, lighting the white candle, sitting on the couch with pen and paper on my lap. I didn't even get counted down the second day before the words began to appear. Basically the message was that I was now going to be an artist. I immediately began to argue and to explain to God that this could not be my mission because I didn't have any education in art or any known talent. I kept explaining to God, "You've got the wrong person." I explained that by "creative" I had meant "not boring"; that I didn't want to spend my days counting other people's money or doing some repetitive action like working in a factory. The message continued as if I weren't arguing for my limitations. I was to purchase watercolors, calligraphy pens, and 8 ½ by 11 parchment paper in various colors and I was to paint greeting cards and market them.

I had $105.00 period in the World and knew nothing about painting or marketing. I had taken six nights of calligraphy lessons while I was still living in Texas. The name of the greeting card company was to be "bj originals, inc." I was instructed that the name was to be all in lower case lettters. The cards were to sell for $2.00 each. The paper was to be folded into thirds. I was appalled, disbelieving and frightened.

I went to an office supply store and purchased a children's set of school watercolors and the parchment paper. The first time I sat down to attempt to paint a flower with a butterfly suspended over it came out of the brush. I was fascinated watching myself do something I didn't know how to do. The messages that were to be in the cards were given to me in the meditation. I made as many cards as I had paper for.

A few days later, I had a call from a man who I had met at a Methodist singles Sunday school and he invited me to go to a psychic fair with him the next day. I had also received an invitation from an ex-lover I hadn't seen in over a year who invited me to fly to Houston to spend some time and figure out what I wanted to do now that I was unemployed. I had accepted and was flying out on Saturday afternoon. I explained to the man who had invited me to the psychic fair that I didn't want to have anything to do with anything psychic, that psychics were strange little old gray-haired ladies who wore shawls and long dangly earrings and burned incense. He confronted me that I didn't know what I was talking about, that there was a lot more to being psychic than fortune telling and he dared me to go.

I agreed to meet him at the university where the psychic fair was being held, but that I would take my own car in case I wanted to leave early and that I had a plane to catch Saturday afternoon. He agreed. I meditated before I went to bed and asked for a concrete sign that what I was contacting was really God. The words came, "When you encounter a huge triangle suspended by three spires of granite you will be sure of the Source of these messages."

I packed and drove to the university to meet my friend and his young son. We first attended a video about Kirlean photography. I realized from the film that psychic energy can be photographed and that there was more to being psychic than fortune telling, but the incense smell was drifting down the hall and my sinuses were acting up because of it. I asked my friend if we could walk outside for a minute so I could clear my head and he agreed. As soon as we stepped out into the quadrangle of the university I spotted a huge bronze triangle supported by three spires of granite. I just about passed out and wet my pants. I had asked for a concrete sign that I was communicating with God and granite was about as concrete as it gets. I was shaken by the sign coming so quickly after I had asked for confirmation of the source of the messages.

We reentered the psychic fair and proceeded to move from table to table. I picked up brochures from each table: one on the *Silva Method of Mind Control*, one on the *Course in Miracles*, and one about *Touch for Health*. I was beginning to feel overwhelmed and told my friend I had to leave for the airport.

I was early for my flight and still a bit shaken by the recent synchronicity so I went into the gift shop in the airport to see if I could find something to send to my children. Right in front of me was the paperback book rack and the first book my eyes fell upon was *The Silva Method of Mind Control*. Even more amazed and dazed I bought the book, went to my gate and began to read the book. The book described a method of getting in touch with one's soul through meditation to receive helpful guidance from the soul. The meditation was almost exactly like the one in the book that had fallen off the shelf in the Walden's bookstore.

I did not explain to my friend in Houston what was happening with me. He was in law enforcement and I didn't think he would believe me. He went to work every day and I continued to paint cards, meditate and read the Silva book. I had agreed to stay in Houston with my friend for ten days, but on the fifth day I was asked in meditation to return to Oklahoma City and to take the Silva Mind Control class. I told my friend I needed to get back to Oklahoma City to get a job because I was uncomfortable being unemployed. He was understanding and took me to the airport and paid to change my ticket.

When I returned home, I called the people who taught Silva about taking the course. I asked how much the course cost and if they took credit cards. The teacher replied that they did take credit cards, but that it would be a month before I could take the class because they had already finished the first weekend of a two weekend class and that they only offered it once a month. I explained to her that I was unemployed and needed to take the course now and inquired if I could learn what the others had learned last weekend and join this class this weekend. She said, "No." But I persisted and asked her to take my number and that if she changed her mind to please call me. After about twenty minutes my phone rang: She admitted that she had gone into meditation and she had been asked to bring herself and the information to my apartment to teach me what the others had learned so I could indeed join the class continuing that weekend. She had never been expected by her soul to offer individual instructions to anyone.

The reason my soul wanted me to take the course was so that I would meet certain others who were practicing meditation to receive information from their souls. I joined a meditation group of Silva graduates who met once a week, where I was destined to later meet my next husband.

After about a week I woke up one morning to rain. I was completely out of cash and only had one credit card left that in an emergency I could charge $285.00. I meditated and the message was to go to go to the neighborhood Albertson's store. I argued, "It's raining outside, I'm not dressed, I haven't showered, my hair's not done and I have no makeup on." The message was repeated over and over. I finally stopped arguing, but didn't get dressed up, pulled on a sweat suit and went to the Albertsons as I was, disgusted at being expected to go out in the rain to a grocery store when I had no money.

I walked through the grocery store with an empty grocery cart wondering how weird things were going to get, wondering if the peas were going to light up and begin to talk to me. After a short time I heard a man's voice say, "What are you doing, I haven't seen you in the longest time?" I turned and looked toward the voice and saw the Rainbow bread man putting bread on the rack. He had often come to my window at the bank to get his check cashed every Friday. How he recognized me out of the bank and in my sweats was a miracle. I replied, "I'm not at the bank anymore."

"I know that. When I go there you haven't been there. What are you doing now?" I hesitated to tell the Rainbow bread man that God had designed a line of greeting cards and was looking for a place to market them.

"I'm painting greeting cards," I said.

"Where do you market them?" he asked.

"I don't know anything about marketing," I admitted.

"You should market them here. There are eight stores in the Oklahoma City metro area and they are open twenty-four hours a day. All the people in charge of marketing in that department are going to be here tomorrow from Tulsa and I can get you an appointment with them and you can show them what you have."

I didn't know what to say. I was flabbergasted. I finally said, "OK."

"Give me your phone number and I'll call you tomorrow with the time and location for you to meet the district manager."

He didn't even write the number down, but assured me he would remember it. He did call and I took a basket with some sample cards to the store he indicated. All the time I was thinking, "This is ridiculous. Marketing a handmade product made by one woman in a national chain store is not good business. Surely this guy is going to laugh in my face."

I was led to the back of the store and met the district manager. He very patiently looked at each card and read each one of them. When he looked up he said, "These are lovely and amazing. We definitely want to carry them, but you will need to furnish the racks as we can't put them on the racks with the national brand cards. You'll need to get eight racks and bring them to the back door of each store, with enough cards to fill them. I'll notify the stores that you are a new vendor. Can you begin bringing them in on Monday?"

I nodded and thanked him, still not believing that he had accepted them. I had no idea where to get racks or how I would pay for them. I returned home and meditated again. I received an impression of the Yellow Pages. When I looked under greeting cards I found the name of a wholesale greeting card company. I called the number and a man answered. I asked if he had any racks that didn't have a company name on them that would fit the dimension of my cards. He began to laugh. I asked why he was laughing. "Lady, I've got them hanging from the rafters. Someone ordered them in 1977 and went out of business before they ever picked them up so I got stuck with them. I can sell them to you for 1977 prices. How many do you need?"

"I will need eight," I replied. "How much will they cost?"

"I can let you have them for $100 a piece."

"When can I pick them up?" I asked.

"I'm going out of town in a little while, but I'll be back and you can pick them up Sunday afternoon if you meet me at my warehouse at one o'clock."

I agreed and hung up the phone and went back into meditation to ask God how I was going to pay for the racks. "Write a check. I'll get you the money before the check gets to the bank on Monday." Once again I was flabbergasted and unbelieving that this was what God really expected of me. I knew if I wrote a hot check for $800 and God didn't cover it that I could never be bonded to be a banker again, the only thin g I was trained to do, and that anything over $700 was considered a felony and I could go to prison.

"*And I would like you to attend a seminar this weekend called The Silva Method of Healing,*" were the words in the meditation. I called the people who taught Silva and asked if the seminar was full and how much it cost. Of course it cost $285, what was left on my only remaining credit card. I registered and showed up on Saturday morning.

During the first lecture I was distracted by seeing a good looking, older white-haired gentleman standing in the doorway to the meeting room.

He looked familiar to me. At the break I went over to him thinking that if I looked at his name tag that I would remember from where I knew him. Standing in front of him and reading his name tag I realized that I didn't know him and was then embarrassed that he would think I was trying to pick him up with the oldest line in the world, "Don't I know you from somewhere?" I excused myself mumbling, "Must have been in another lifetime." I didn't even believe in past lives at this point, but I just wanted to get away. I returned to my seat and bowed my head still embarrassed. He soon came over to where I was sitting and asked if he could take me to lunch and that maybe in talking we could figure out where we knew each other from. I didn't have enough money left to buy my lunch so it seemed like a good idea that he take me to lunch.

At lunch I showed him the greeting card samples and told him about the messages I received. He was impressed and admitted that he was now retired and attempting to do what was happening to me. He asked if he could take me to lunch again the next day, but I told him I needed to pick up racks for my greeting cards and would be late getting back to the seminar. I did not tell him I did not have the money or that I was writing an insufficient check. He said he would save me a seat made me promise to come and sit with him when I returned and I agreed.

Writing the hot check was one of the most difficult things I've ever done. I was so tense when I returned to the seminar that I could not talk. The speaker had already begun so I quickly took my seat beside the man who was expecting me to sit with him. He smiled as I took my seat and soon placed his hand on my leg under the table and leaned over and in a very loud whisper asked, "Did you get your racks?" He was wearing hearing aids so I soon realized he had no idea how loud he was "whispering." I was so scared I was mute. He said it again even louder, "Did you get your racks?" I had not told him that I did not have the money and that I was going to pay for them with a hot check. I turned to him and nodded to indicate that I had purchased the racks. He then said in his loud whisper, "How much did they cost?" I thought "that is my business that is God's business, I don't know you and get your hand off my leg," but again I was too scared to even talk. Again he repeated his loudly whispered question, "How much did they cost?" I wrote $800.00 on a piece of paper and shoved it over to him to try to get him to shut up. In a few minutes he took my hand under the table and put paper in my hand. I felt relieved that we were going to write notes instead of loudly whispering and letting everyone in the room know that I had committed a felony.

When the speaker quit I took my hand out from under the table and opened it. He had filled my hand with hundred dollar bills. I pointed at the money and stammered, "What is this?"

He replied, "It's money."

"Well I see that, but why are you putting it in my hand? I can't borrow it from you. I have no collateral and I don't know if I will ever make enough money to give it back to you."

"Who asked you to give it back? You don't understand; before I left Texas to come up here for this seminar my soul asked me to go to my safety deposit box and take out eight $100 bills and bring them with me. I never carry cash with me when I travel; I always use credit cards. I realized this morning when I woke up that Spirit has been showing me an image of you in my dreams for weeks and that is why I thought I recognized you. I never watch TV other than for the news, but a week before I came to Oklahoma City I sat in the middle of the floor for four nights and watched a movie called *The Thorn Birds* and cried with frustration for the priest in the movie who was in love with a woman he could not have. When you told me the story about your priest friend yesterday at lunch I realized that he was contacting me through the movie to lead me here to help you."

I began to cry. He put his arms around me and assured me that he was gladly giving me the money to help me to get the business started that God wanted to create through me and that he couldn't do what I was doing, but that he was sure he was to help. He took my phone number and left to return to Texas to his wife.

I covered the check, put the racks and cards in each store on Monday and was appalled to find out that I would not be given a check for six weeks because it would take that long for them to set me up as a new vendor through their home office in Salt Lake City. I had to begin to borrow 10, 20 and 30 dollars from people I hardly knew to buy the paper and envelopes to continue. I had to paint twenty hours a day to keep up with the sales. I was suffering from sleep deprivation and fear when one morning the phone rang and woke me.

Groggily I said, "Hello."

"How are you doing?" my benefactor's cheerful voice inquired.

"Not well. I've created a monster and I can't paint fast enough to feed it," I blurted.

I explained to him that they had not paid me for the cards and wouldn't be paying me for at least six weeks when I would be set up on their computers as a new vendor and that I was of necessity borrowing money to buy the paper and envelopes from people I hardly knew.

"Haven't you gotten your photocopy machine yet?" he asked.

Sleep deprivation is not a pretty sight; I completely lost it and started yelling at him, "You stupid son of a bitch you've obviously never been broke in your life. I'm borrowing money for paper, I'm behind on all my bills and have no money for food or gas and you think I can buy a photocopy machine that costs several thousand dollars?" Sleep deprivation and fear had made me crazy.

"Calm down, calm down, I'm coming to Oklahoma City tomorrow to see a doctor there and I'm supposed to buy you a photocopy machine so you can do the calligraphy on a white sheet of paper and then photocopy the words onto the parchment paper and you can paint twice as many cards and they will still look hand printed."

I was taken aback by his offer and thought, "Maybe I can get the price of my body up so I can comfortably negotiate it later or this man really is being sent by God or Edward and I'm too tired and scared now to argue."

"What time will you arrive?" I asked.

"I'll leave early and get there in time to take you for lunch. Why don't you go down today and find the right machine and then we can just go purchase it after lunch and get you started using it," he suggested.

"OK. I'll see you around noon." I sat back against the head of the bed stunned and confused wondering if Edward was influencing this man or was God. I was too tired to care.

That afternoon I dressed and went downtown to a business machine store and watched a demonstration of various copy machines and chose the one the salesman thought would work best for what I needed. Bill, the man from the seminar, arrived about noon. We went to lunch and then purchased the machine. We brought it to my apartment in the trunk of his car. As we were standing before it reading the manual and figuring out how to use it, he asked me about my financial situation.

"My credit cards are all maxed out, my bills and rent are all past due and I have no money for food, gas or paper and envelopes," I confessed.

"Give me your credit cards," he more or less demanded. I knew I could not legally continue to use them and figured he was going to take them to keep me from trying to use them and getting into trouble so I gave them to him.

He left and I thought he went on to the doctor and left for his return to Texas, but about two hours later I heard a knock on the door and there he was. He handed me the cards and receipts where he had gone to the bank and paid off $4,000.00 in credit cards so I could continue to fulfill my obligations to Albertson's and pay my bills. Once again I began to cry from exhaustion and relief.

He also handed me a miniature cassette tape recorder and explained that Spirit had indicated that he should stop at the Radio Shack and buy the tape recorder for me, because I was going to write some books that I would speak the information into the tape recorder and someone else would type it up for me. I had been given the request in meditation that I would be expected to write books in the future, but felt as limited about writing books as I had about painting and marketing. I had been assured by Spirit that, "Bach will help you." I had no idea what that meant other than the book I had purchased when I left Texas was written by Richard Bach and I certainly had no idea how I would ever meet him.

I gratefully accepted the recorder and credit cards and his help. He then asked," What are we supposed to do now?" "While you were gone I meditated and Spirit suggested that I go to Hurst, Texas to do a healing on a woman's heart there. I met a woman in the lobby at the Silva seminar who has a daughter who lives in Hurst who is facing heart surgery. The woman asked me what I do and I showed her the greeting cards and she said her daughter has started a greeting card company with cards that are almost identical to the ones I've created. Her daughter's company is called dr originals, all lower case letters, and the paper, envelopes and messages are almost identical to the ones I created only she is a pen and ink artist that made hers easier to reproduce."

He suggested I call the mother of the woman in Hurst and ask her if her daughter would be receptive to having me visit. I did and she indicated she had spoken with her daughter who said she would love to meet me. Bill said he was on his way to Dallas to visit his cousin so I could ride with him and that he would buy me a one way ticket to return to Oklahoma after I had met with her. On the way to Dallas, I read him some of the cosmic information I had received in meditation. When we were approaching Dallas he asked if I would be willing to go to dinner with him and his cousin. He thought it would be a good idea for me to meet his cousin, because he had been a member of the national board of the Church of Religious Science, had taken the Silva Method, meditated and was a professional artist. I agreed and we went to dinner. His cousin was an interesting man and asked me lots of questions about how I had begun to meditate and receive messages. He admitted he had not been meditating recently, but that after meeting me he would once again begin to meditate. At the end of the evening he said, "I have a cousin I think would really like to meet you."

"Where does your cousin live?" I asked.

"He lives in California," he replied.

"Well, I'm never going to California. My car wouldn't even make it to Dallas so I had to ride with Bill. My car currently uses more oil than it does gas."

"What is your cousin's name?" I asked.

"His name is Marcus Bach," he answered.

"Really, do you think he has any connection to Richard Bach?" I asked.

"Marcus is Richard's uncle," he said.

"What does Marcus do for a living?" I asked

"He writes metaphysical books for Unity Church," he answered.

"In that case you had better give me the information maybe I can communicate with him by mail."

He wrote out the information and Bill took me to Diana Roger's apartment.

When he dropped me off he said it would be the last time we would see each other or be in communication, since he knew his personality well enough to know that if we continued to see each other he would begin to expect us to have a sexual relationship. He knew that was not what our relationship was to be about. He kissed me on the cheek; drove away and never contacted me again.

Diana and I fell into easy conversation and she suggested I go to bed early. The next day I did the energy transfer into her heart. I had panicked my way through the seminar dealing with Bill, buying the racks and writing the hot check, so I remembered very little of what the speaker had said about doing healing, but Diana reminded me that my job was to transfer the energy and that her job was to use it.

I flew back to Oklahoma City the next day. That next weekend I attended the local Science of Mind Church that Bill's cousin had recommended was a place I would meet other people who meditate. I was standing in the church gift shop looking at the book rack when a man I had met at the Silva class spoke to me. He asked, "Have you read this book?" He showed me a copy he had just purchased of a book called *The World of Serendipity* written by Marcus Bach. I started to laugh and explained that I had just met Marcus' cousin in Dallas.

"I don't have time to read the book right now, why don't you take it and read it and return it to me when you come to meditation next week," he suggested.

I gratefully took the book and read it that afternoon and painted and wrote several cards and mailed them to Marcus. The cards were taken from a saying he had used in his book. "Thanks to chance you came my way. Three cheers for serendipity." Years later, when I finally did go to California, I met Marcus and his lovely wife and he still had the cards in his filing system. He was not willing, however, to help me with writing or to introduce me to his nephew Richard. Maybe Spirit meant the music of Bach, the composer or maybe Marcus didn't understand the significance of Spirit's message, or maybe I will still meet Richard or, since Marcus is now in the World of Spirit, maybe he will help me from there.

I married the man from the meditation group and the marriage lasted for nine months as it was supposed to. My son came to live with me for that nine months and attended school. Since my husband had a son approximately the same age and he daily made breakfast for the boys and took them to and from school, I was free to meditate and paint.

In 1994 the Master Jesus materialized in my bedroom one morning and asked me to start a non-profit organization called Namaste, Inc. I had no idea how to start a non-profit organization, but agreed to do it. He intimated that He and I would hold an umbrella of energy under which twelve Namaste retreat centers would be formed. I was stunned and again felt inadequate.

After nine months, my husband asked me for a divorce. He found he could not comfortably live with someone who was psychic even though when I met him he claimed to be psychic himself. I was asked by Spirit to sell the greeting card company that I had been running for three years. The afternoon of the day I received the message in meditation to sell the greeting card company, a woman called on the phone to ask if I had ever considered selling the card company and that she and her partner were interested in purchasing it. They came by that afternoon with the check and purchased it. I was then asked to give up the house I had been renting, put my belongings in storage and let my son return to his father for the summer. It was suggested that I keep only what would fit in the car, I begin to travel and every day in meditation I would be given the name of the town to drive to and the names of the people I was suppose to find to deliver messages to from the person's soul.

I was intimidated and once again depressed, but followed the suggestions. I soon found that calling strangers and saying that God had given me their name in meditation and could I come by to deliver a message from their soul was the worst cold call anyone would ever be asked to make. The people would either hang up on me, or want to meet me at the Denny's to see what kind of a kook I was, or some would gratefully say, "I asked for a channel two weeks ago, what took you so long to get here?" Those people would take me home with them and take care of me, feed me and let me sleep on their couch for a few days and sometimes even introduce me to other people I had on my list of people to find. I traveled for three months believing that I would return to Oklahoma City after the summer, rent another home and the children would come back to live with me. Instead, the soul asked me to allow the children to remain in Texas, for me to return to Oklahoma City, sell all my belongings from storage and to continue to travel. I was assured by my soul that in the future, when I once again had a house everything I needed would be provided.

I did what was suggested. It was difficult to watch people carry my belongings away from the garage sale, but I did it. Freed from the responsibility of a home and belongings, I continued to travel for several years as a homeless person, driving from one state to another, building my faith muscles and meeting interesting people. I met a woman in Denver named Judi; we are from the same Oversoul. Years later, Judi was asked by our Oversoul to refinance her home in Denver to purchase a place in Oklahoma City for me to have a Namaste retreat center. She followed her guidance and I moved into the center in 2002.

The day she called to tell me about the message she had received, I must have been smiling more than usual, because the man behind the counter noticed and asked me why I seemed so happy. I told him, "I am finally going to have my own home." He reached into his shirt pocket and retrieved a business card and handed it to me. He said, "Maybe I can help you with that since I just passed my real estate exam."

He came to the house I was renting that afternoon and looked at my manifestation book where I had listed what I was looking for in a place to live and use for a retreat center. He told me he knew of the place, but that he didn't want to show it to me because it was a repossessed home and was currently being redone. I assured him I would know as soon as I saw it if it was the right place. I had an arrangement with my soul that when I needed confirmation, the soul would materialize a blue feather. Sure enough, when we approached the front door of the house, there was a blue feather. In 2002 Judi bought the house and I moved in.

A few years later, Judi moved to Oklahoma City to join in working with me. We found a perfect home for her overlooking the river one-half block from the center.

2.

Communication With Mother

In 1986 I was asked by my soul to go to Sedona, Arizona. When I drove into town it was suggested that I keep driving through town and go to a KOA campground just west of town. I followed the suggestion, even though I was certainly not prepared or willing to camp out. When I arrived at the campground the suggestion was to enter the clubhouse of the campground, which I did. As I entered the building, I noticed that the room was mostly empty; the only occupants being two older ladies sitting at a table in the corner drinking iced tea. I moved toward the coke machine, trying to display a reason for entering the room. The women looked up and began to wave for me to join them. I looked behind me, assuming they were waving at someone else who must be standing behind me. No one was there. I pointed at my chest to visually indicate, "You mean me?" They nodded their heads in unison and once again waved to indicate, "Come here". I moved in their direction.

They introduced themselves as Honey Lee French (who has since become the accountant for Namaste), and a woman named Jackie. "What took you so long to get here?" Jackie asked. Flustered, and still believing they had me confused with someone else, I mumbled, "I've been driving all day from Albuquerque."

"We've been sitting here since noon, drowning ourselves in iced tea, waiting for you," Honey Lee added.

"How did you know I was coming? Are you sure I'm the person you are expecting?" I queried.

"Oh, yes, we're sure. Spirit told me you would arrive today," Jackie answered.

"Really?" I managed. This was my first experience that Spirit had told anyone I encountered that I was coming to see them.

"Yes, really. Now sit down and tell us what you've been up to," Honey Lee responded.

All evening we shared stories. Honey Lee had just returned from an amazing Spirit led journey to Alaska. Jackie's husband, I learned, was a medium who drew pastel portraits of a person's spirit guide. I left them at midnight agreeing to return the next morning to have Jackie's husband, Stan, draw a picture of my spirit guide. On my drive into Sedona I argued with my guidance. "I know what you look like. I know who you are. Why should I spend money I need for other things to get a portrait of you, which I have no space for in my van lifestyle?" The argument was useless. The guidance was clear. "You will keep the appointment."

The next morning I returned to the campground. The ladies were making breakfast on a camp stove and invited me to join them, which I did. They were both great cooks. After breakfast, Jackie said, "Stan is expecting you. Just go tap on the door of the trailer and he's ready when you are to do your spirit portrait."

I made my way around the fifth-wheel trailer and knocked on the door with great trepidation and resistance, still muttering under my breath at my guidance. The door opened and I stepped back almost falling off the steps. The odor from inside the trailer was ominous. The man who opened the door reminded me the drawings in a children's book of Ichibod Crane. He was well over six feet tall, had a hooked nose, was thin as a rail and wore a black suit and white shirt. He had an obviously hastily applied toupee sitting crosswise on his head. I had to stifle a laugh. My interior thoughts were rampant. "This is by far the dumbest thing you have ever asked me to do. What in God's name is this about?"

He invited me to enter the trailer. He preceded me down the aisle. The place was packed from floor to ceiling with their belongings and smelled of stale air, unwashed body odor, and rancid cooking smells. The wonderful breakfast I had just consumed threatened to come up. Taking a deep breath to calm my stomach was out of the question. Instead, I held my breath and proceeded to the chair he indicated in the small area where his easel was set up at the front of the trailer by an open window. I was so grateful for the whiff of fresh air. Stan introduced himself and said he would say a prayer to connect himself to my soul and would begin to draw. He explained that I need not do anything, that my presence was enough. I spent the time he was praying, continuing the interior dialogue with my soul and complaining about being there.

Stan began to draw an image of an Indian chief with a full headdress. He explained to me that my guide's name was Red Cloud and that he had been a very brave warrior and leader. I thought, "My God, this guy is a fraud. Not only do I have to endure this place and spend the money, this guy is not even going to be accurate. How am I going to get out of this? Why do I have to do this? Where am I going to keep a fragile pastel picture of an Indian, who isn't even my guide, in my van?" I tried not to groan. I tried to just admire his artistic abilities, even though what he was drawing in no way related to me.

Suddenly his eyes filled with tears and he stopped drawing and looked directly at me. "What's the matter?" I asked.

"A Mother energy just entered the room," he responded.

"It's probably Lady Master Venus, she's my galactic mother or maybe Lady Nada, Mother of the World. I'm usually in contact with both of them. It's probably not the Mother Mary. I seldom communicate with her," I nervously rushed it all together.

"No, she says she's your Mother," he replied almost in a whisper.

"Well, I don't need to talk with her. What I don't need is a lecture about my lifestyle," I told him. I thought to myself, "I don't have much to worry about anyway, he's a fraud, and is certainly not going to really be able to talk with anyone that I would actually know."

"She says she understands how you feel. She's determined that you would really believe it is her before she gives you the real message she has for you. She says she was allergic to all things when she was in her body: perfumes, flowers, cigarettes, cleaning products and all forms of fabric except cotton. She says she had to make all her own clothing and that all her clothing had to be cotton. She says that she was allergic to cleaning supplies and all petroleum products and most foods", he said all this with his eyes closed and with tears streaming down his face.

I was overwhelmed with his information, as it was all an accurate description of my Mother's life. I began to cry. "OK, what does she want to say? I'll listen to whatever it is." He was obviously in touch with my Mother's energy even though he was obviously not in touch with my guide.

"She says there is one more thing she has to tell you to convince you it is really her. She is concerned you won't believe her message, because she says it is so different than how she was with you when you were together; so different than what she believed was important when she lived on Earth."

"She says to remember the red rose. She says once, on your twenty-first birthday, that you had the florist send her a single red rose in a vase."

I began to cry even harder. I had overheard a friend say she had sent her mother flowers on her birthday to thank her mother for birthing her. I thought, "What a thoughtful idea, but my Mother is allergic to flowers." But I chose to send the one rose anyway, thinking my gratitude will be conveyed and if she can't stand it she can throw it away, keep it outside or in the refrigerator. I ordered the flower and had it delivered. My Mother mentioned receiving the flower, but never spoke of it extensively, which at the time disappointed me.

At the time of her death, my sister-in-law and I cleaned out her drawers and closets for my father. We found the rose, note, greenery and vase, wrapped in a whole roll of aluminum foil, in the bottom of my Mother's lingerie drawer. Tapped to the side of the bundle was a note in my Mother's hand writing that read, "Receiving this rose fulfilled a lifetime fantasy."

"Yes, I remember, go ahead," I managed to utter through my sobs.

"She says she is proud of you. That what you are doing, traveling and delivering messages, particularly the message that a person's spirit does not die, is the single most important thing a person can do. That delivering that message is more important than motherhood, being a wife or a grandmother. She wants you to know that she approves of what you are doing and have done. She says that she's sorry that she did not tell you when she was alive how proud of you she was, how much she admired you or how proud she was of the way you kept your home, took care of your children, your husband and still had time to help her and to work at the church. She's sorry she always seemed critical of you. She says she's proud of you for getting off the Valium. That she wishes she had been strong enough not to take so many drugs. She wants you to know she will be with you when you are lonely and traveling by yourself. She also says she is sorry about giving Peanut away."

"'Remember, most of all, that I'm proud of you,' that's her message," he opened his eyes.

I was speechless, shivering and sobbing. I could hardly believe what I had just heard, through this bizarre man with the crooked toupee, who I considered a fraud, in this cluttered, dirty place. My Mother must indeed have been desperate to get her message through to me.

Years later, while reading the *Texas* magazine, I heard her voice myself. "This is a picture of where I am. This is Summerland." My mother loved sitting on the porch, she loved flowers, although she couldn't have them. I could see how this home she had created would indeed be her idea of heaven. I smiled and thought, "Good for you, Mom."

3.
Communication With John in the Afterlife

In 2001 my ex-husband, my children's Father, the one I left when I moved to Oklahoma, was killed in an automobile accident on his way here to our grandson's second birthday party. We were all devastated by the loss. He appeared in many ways to all of us during the first year, by moving objects, through music, dreams and through memories and thoughts that would be planted in our minds when we were together. After the first year he began to appear to me and to encourage me to apply for his social security. I did not know that I would qualify for his social security, since he had remarried. I did not knowingly have his social security number. He kept assuring me I should apply and that the number was in the "pink book". I didn't have any idea what "pink book" he meant. One day a friend told me that I did qualify for his social security if we had been married for more than ten years. I was amazed that both his most recent wife and I would both draw from his social security without impinging on each other's benefits.

One day I was searching for something in my office closet when my eye fell upon an outdated address book that was probably 20 years old. It was pink. I looked up my ex-husband's name and sure enough under his name was his social security number. I called and made an appointment with the social security office. The reason I had not been encouraged by him sooner to apply was that technically I did not qualify to receive it until I was sixty years old, which I had just become. The benefits were established and I began to receive them within a month. He explained to me that he felt he owed me the benefits because he had not made more of an effort to understand my needs and me when we were married. He seemed relieved of his burden of guilt once the income was in place. He now only approaches me when he feels he is trying to get a message to one of the children and he isn't getting through to them.

4.

Death: Life's Greatest Adventure

It is better to avoid sin than to fear death.

For death to be so universal and vital an experience, it seems incredible that Humans know so little about it, not only the actual experience of death itself, but what happens on the other side. This experience lies inevitably in the future for all of us.

Death is simply a change in vibration. Physical forms vibrate at a certain rate of vibration amenable to that of Earth. As long as we inhabit a form vibrating at that rate of speed, we will be able to see Earth, people and all material objects. Death is an alteration of speed or vibration. Discarding the physical form so that the consciousness may accommodate itself to a form with altered frequency usually requires a pause in consciousness while the soul is discarding a body vibrating at a slow wave length, and is becoming conscious of inhabiting a form of higher substance. So that the transfer from one vibration to another can be gentle, there usually is an intermediate state of consciousness. It is the Self's built-in anesthesia for the Soul's transition, not to deaden pain, rather to cushion any shock entailed in entering a world of increased vibrational frequency.

Thoughts associated with death are, for most people dark, foreboding, fear filled and dreaded. To a few it represents a release from pain and affliction, even though they believe it to be a state of non-existence. To many it means a long sleep, awaiting the end of the World, resurrection and Judgment Day. Death is just a process of transition; a birth from the Earth plane and the womb of the physical form, into a new and better world with a new and better form. It is terrifying to many because, when viewed from our normal level of perception it seems to be the "unknown."

Death is a natural process, it has an automatic beginning. As soon as the Human form attains its physical maturity, when the spirit finally assumes full control, that form begins the natural process of death. The body does not die suddenly, unless through accident; it only seems to. Although the change is imperceptible, the transition proceeds over many years. The form gradually relinquishes its powers and faculties as the soul within gradually assume them.

Beginning in adulthood, the soul is no longer traveling an involving descending arc as it did in the early part of the incarnation. It turns toward evolving. It enters the arc of spiritual ascendancy. Its tendencies reach toward the worlds of spirit. The normal process of death begins around the age of twenty-one when the form has gained its physical maturity and fulfilled its etheric pattern. The mind continues to unfold, to grow, to mature, enabling the personality to become older but wiser.

As maturity advances to old age, the physical form succumbs to subtle natural changes. Just as the soul prepares itself for another incarnation on Earth prior to its birth into the physical form, so does the soul require preparation for death and withdrawal from that form. Birth is far more than issuing a physical form out of the mother's womb and into physical manifestation. It is true, the first breath begins the inflow of the individualized life stream at that time, but the soul does not complete its union with the personality before the seventh year, and is frequently still in the process until the twenty-first year. The preparation for withdrawal of the soul takes place gradually. The aging body only indicates that specific changes are occurring in the corporeal organism, the better to prepare the soul for its coming travel into a higher plane.

Many accept eternal life academically and intellectually, but have not truly grasped the full significance of its utter reality. When we do, when we consider that we enter and leave numerous organic bodies in the full sweep of our eternal journey, death assumes its rightful place. The dread terror subsides. Old age fails to frighten us and we even experience illnesses with less apprehension.

Old age is a great deal more than the slowing down processes of the physical form. These are only outer indications of an inner process. When this inner gradation begins, the physical organs react accordingly. The soul, continually developing and expanding its faculties, begins to extend them as intuitive feelers toward the higher spheres. It is the gradual strengthening of the soul which causes the apparent deterioration of the physical form because the soul is taking unto itself the vitality it once shared with the body.

As the soul begins to absorb more and more of the vital energies necessary for its unfoldment and withdrawal, the body reacts to its decreasing supply of life force. Atom after atom slips away in an imperceptible emanation from the physical body, like slow falling sand in an hourglass. Instead of being replaced in the physical, these departing atoms are transmuted to take their place in the soul body.

It should not be thought that this spiritual body is something apart, awaiting somewhere aloft our time of demise. It is a body of atomic essence, even now permeating the physical form. The two are coexistent. Every experience of the mortal influences and molds the spiritual from within. While the physical requires food and drink and warmth and shelter, the spiritual form finds its sustenance in thought force. If the desires are degenerate, the atoms will form a shell of astral darkness over the soul. If the thoughts are beautiful, the astral form will shine with a starry radiance. Its food is purity, goodness, truth and wisdom. Therefore, though a Human may be wealthy materially, they may be poor in spirit. For one to nurture the spiritual to perfection, they must seek education and instruction in spiritual things.

Often old age turns into senility. The faculties of intellect which were once alert become weak, clouded by both physical and mental decline. The brilliance once in evidence departs. It is usually true that the older one grows physically the more they grow in spiritual perfection. As the flame of earthly passions abate, the dying embers kindle the fires of a new love, that of the spirit. The debris of a lifetime drops away. Old hates mellow, old ambitions fade. Many live among the memories of bygone years in their normal waking consciousness, while their spiritual consciousness unfolds like a rosebud opening to full bloom.

The detraction of the physical form only indicates the vitalizing of the inner spiritual form. Even though one may be outwardly aware of their inner spiritual expansion and even though their physical self only exhibits senility and loss of mental acumen, still their inner awareness is tending heavenward. The intuitive faculties often perceive a gradual expansion of psychic awareness.

Those who die in the prime of life, possessing the firmness and beauty of youth, sometimes require long to build an equal beauty in spiritual form. But to grow old in physical age is usually to grow into spiritual youth. Physical deformities are not reflected in the spiritual form. (If there are deformities, they are of the soul.) Many a plain exterior covers a spiritual form of beauty. Good thoughts, good deeds and a search for wisdom confer blessings and grace upon the spiritual features. However feeble the physical, however old and wrinkled, the truly good are always spiritually beautiful.

Frequently it is difficult for the liberated soul to understand that there has been a transition. Many think they are experiencing a vivid dream. They realize they are very much alive, that their bodies are perfect in structure and function; they hear with their ears and see with their eyes and speak with their lips. They behold friends who had previously crossed. Yet it sometimes requires a fleeting period of time to become fully convinced that it is not all a heavenly dream. Once conviction becomes certain, the joy of reunion is beyond Human description.

THERE IS A COSMIC CLOCK OF DESTINY

Before our last physical birth, while we still resided in the realms of the unseen, we decided that it was time to make another journey to Earth. At that time, we knew the highlights of our mission. We also knew how long we would remain. The timing of our coming and our future departure was set on a great cosmic clock, not a clock as we know it, but a built-in timer in our own cosmic nervous system; a timer set to affinity-vibrations.

At birth the soul merged with the body through electromagnetic hold and that attraction was set for release by a certain cosmic affinity. When the time arrives for the body to release its electromagnetic hold upon the soul, the two will separate. We call such a separation death. The time of the release is the moment we will die, not one second sooner or one second later; neither disease, war nor accident can change the timing of the vibration lock. There have been known to be extensions granted by the soul for some exceptional spiritual purpose, but these are rare exceptions to the Law. It is possible to request a life extension if one is here on a spiritual mission and feels they have not as yet fulfilled their mission. Suicides disrupt the natural process of this Law, reaping their own karmic retribution.

When the karmic time of this incarnation has run out and the death hormones, which signal departure, are released, the soul turns toward the spheres from which it came at the time of birth.

Humanity divides itself into three categories:
1. The animal-like Human who live the Earth life principally through the senses; this is the degenerate.
2. The soul-like Human who divides their interests between

gratification of the senses and satisfying mental conquests; this is the average Human;
3. The Spiritual Human who recognizes the illusion of the sense world, and seeks to use spiritual perception to its fullest; this is the initiate.

The degenerates, after death, having discounted the spiritual world, will view their place on the astral through considerably limited vision and perception. Because they have only known Earthly and animalistic sensations, their thoughts turn constantly Earthward, and they are drawn through vibrational attractions to that which gave them sensual pleasure on the Earth. They enter a world very much patterned after their Earth World. Their channels of higher perception usually remain closed and they often live out their time between incarnations unaware of the real spiritual World and its sublime attributes lying all about them just as they did live out their Earth life unaware of the Otherworld interpenetrating their own.

Often the degenerates are unaware of the inhabitants of the upper realms. They are infant souls, dwelling on a plane and in substance unfamiliar to them. Occasionally, such a soul will reincarnate within a few days after death. They may be caught in the maelstrom of the after death transitional state called *the Bardo (a Tibetan word for "between lives.")* More often they will spend time in purgatory, eventually ascending through the higher planes only briefly. Since all souls, even degenerates, seldom live out a lifetime without doing some good, such a person may eventually attain some awareness of the causal plane, the heaven World, just prior to their descent into another physical birth.

Awakening on the causal is different for every individual. A great many degenerates will choose to be drawn back to Earth long before reaching the causal state of consciousness. For those who do attain it, the awakening or return to consciousness on that plane will be brief. The awareness will open only to a vague subliminal glimpse of the supreme glory of the soul's true home. Such a causal experience will seem more like a sleep and a forgetting, for the degenerate will not have developed sufficient mind power to awaken to full potential on the causal level.

The average Human's after death state is altogether different. For the average Human, death is a natural continuance. Life on the inner planes will follow much the same pattern as their Earthly endeavors. That is, their inner problems will still exist, their ambitions, their loves, their dreams, their hopes and their talents. There will still be much for them to overcome.

But they will pause in the illusion land of the astral long enough to rest their consciousness from turmoil's just ended on the Earth. When their windows of perception begin to open, and their mental muscles feel the need of greater challenge, they will travel upward, out of that illusion land of the astral.

The average Human lives their lives on Earth suspended between two mysteries: the mystery of birth and the mystery of death. But, unlike the degenerate, they find time to consider particularly the Afterlife. It is the development of their own mind power, however focused upon ambitions of Earth and faced with the fierce run of competition that prevents them from ever giving full consideration to the ultimate purpose of their Earth life. There is so little time for leisure or the pursuit of philosophy, because their lives are filled with chaos and busyness. Their lives contain a measure of joy, a measure of sorrow and a full portion of petty, irritating problems that seem bent on preventing what might have been a search for truth.

Most Humans form some idea of the after death state according to the training given by their parents or church leaders. Depending on the religion or philosophy they are exposed to, they determine that there is immortality and an afterlife, or they will believe that they go down to the grave to enter the long sleep and await millenniums for the Second Coming, the end of the World and Judgment Day, or believe they become nonexistent.

Average Humans either realize the absurdity of eternal damnation, or face death fear-filled with the possibility of such an indictment for themselves.

The Spiritual Humans who have focused some attention on using their intuition and not just the World of the senses is more prepared for death with less fear. Their after death state is a continuation of much that they are. They are still the ordinary individual, except that some of the blinders that limited their vision and understanding on Earth are removed.

Even so, they are not transformed in the twinkling of an eye. The transition is only in their form. Like the degenerate, they must not be ushered too suddenly into too high a vibration. They will not have developed the spiritual strength to bear it. Most Spiritual Humans pass into the unseen World, longing to know, but frightened of the potential. They remain in the limited consciousness state of the astral so they may rest in a World very much like their Earth life only until their awakening spiritual perception feels the need of wider horizons. Then their soul development will take them higher. Spiritual advancement is gradual and spiritual awareness increases progressively.

Having discarded their physical forms, their minds are no longer harnessed by the brain cells and the intricate web of nerves constituting the cerebrospinal system through which they communicated on Earth. Their consciousness, expanding with amazing new freedom, learns the flexibility of their new form and how to use it to conform to higher dimensions. Because the Spiritual Human has developed soul qualities, their tenure in the unseen realms will be mostly in the realms of the soul, removed from the lower planes of the degenerate.

In this land, the soul perceives only that to which the person has opened their consciousness during their Earthly sojourn. They will see beauty all about them, for beauty is all that exists there, but they will see only that to which their perceptions and faculties have developed to perceive. So it is on the soul levels of the high astral.

Humans who have opened wider doors of perception through meditation and study will recognize themselves in a "new World." On the lower mental plane they become aware that their form is somewhat changed. They might be compared to the butterfly that retains some portion of its caterpillar form. There are many similarities between the Spiritual Human's old and new forms, yet surrounding the new are billowing colors, lights and shapes. Just as the butterfly takes on different shapes and hues and colors, so does the Human's new mental form. It will assume symmetry and color according to the influence of the soul's karmic past. Thus it may transcend Earth's most indescribable Beauty or it may assume bizarre or grotesque patterns, according to the thoughts that have dominated their deeper consciousness.

They begin to realize that they no longer see simply through their eyes, but with their entire form; that they no longer hear only with their ears, but must adjust their consciousness to accommodate thought waves that strike their entire form. They quickly discover that on this plane the mind and its power far transcends that of form. Here, if one is to accomplish great things, they must control great mental power. They must learn not only how to project it, but how to manipulate it for their own creative happiness. They must learn how to accommodate their life according to the flow of thought waves, for their new world is constructed of thought waves.

In appearance, this World somewhat resembles that of Earth, except that its solids seem fluidic enough to respond to mind power. They quickly become aware of the Law of Vibration and realize that their wellbeing hinges on their awareness of vibrations. On this lower mental plane the intense emotions are given life force. That is, if they loved someone deeply on Earth, that love will be immeasurably enhanced on the mental plane. But the same is true of hate or anger. If a person has an old enemy on Earth, when they both arrive in the Otherworld the emotion of hate will inevitably draw them together, and there, unless they have learned to transcend such negative emotion, they engage in a mental battle much as they would a fist fight on Earth.

In this World the Spiritual Human again knows pain, but not the pain experienced in their physical form. Their pain is that which can only be experienced in the mind, sorrow not connected with grief of Earth, a spiritual sorrow. This is why it is so important that we, while still in physical form, overcome our negative emotions. If we cannot love, it is important to develop indifference rather than hatred.

That is why the word and action of forgiveness is so important on Earth. Hating an enemy for what they have done to you places one in a vibrational level with their hatred and the conflict can bring suffering on the mental plane; if one can forgive while yet on Earth, the tie will be severed. The one actively engaged in hate is the one with the problem. The one who refuses to be drawn into retaliation and revenge really has no problem. They have risen above the level of hate thought currents and are not subject to these destructive energies.

On the mental plane one does not suffer pain and pleasure, happiness and despair in their form, only in their mind. Here, people quickly become aware that if they do not think right they create their own mental suffering, just as they did on Earth. The soul on this plane can experience love far beyond the ecstasies of Earth. One becomes aware quickly that if they are to be happy here they must radiate happiness to others.

After a while the peace and contentment of the higher World may grow tedious and one may begin to desire challenges and struggle. Even freedom from necessities, the soul becomes aware of extreme limitations. Such freedom from desires and with so much freedom one can yearn for some kind of struggle and the contest of challenges, some ecstasy of reward to be experienced.

Freed from the heavy bonds of the flesh, and with increased mental powers, one may become aware that while incarnated they did not take full advantage of the opportunities offered. A person may become aware that they cannot ascend higher until they have mastered the inner conflicts created while they were incarnated. With this awareness a person may choose to reincarnate.

It is important that we learn that regardless of what we own, these possessions are not truly ours, but ours to steward. They belong to the World of matter. The moment we depart this life our possessions cease to be ours and become someone else's. Learn to think in terms of eternity. Learn to possess without being possessed.

In an initiate's Otherworld they learn how to use their minds constructively, molding the tenuous mental substance to the betterment of their life; how to control the mental substance and give it life force.

Initiates may choose to become members of a spiritual group unit or specialized groups that then encourage and inspire Humans who are also involved in their specialization. These are referred to as Group Minds. These groups may be of healers, inventors, musicians, artists, or researchers. There are too many varied groups to enumerate them all.

The initiate, disciple or adept may also choose to reincarnate to help the Spiritual Hierarchy from a Human form to further the spiritual evolution of Humanity.

5.

Dimensions

Jesus is said to have said *"In my Father's house are many mansions. If it were not so I would have told you."* (John 14:2) My soul says this idea was mis- translated and should read "dimensions" instead of mansions. Dimensions refers to the various planes and spheres into which Humanity is separated in order to accommodate the diversities of Humans so that all races and states of consciousness will be "at home" after physical death and between incarnations.

Where, then, can these "other dimensions" be? What people live there? The Master is reported to have said that his disciples would "live also" and would join Him where He dwelt. I believe He was teaching of life after death and the unseen spiritual planes that lie all about us.

On a clear, cloudless night we can reverently survey the immensity of God's stellar world. Easily discernible is a vast belt of "stardust" we call the Milky Way. The dictionary describes this blazing area as "countless millions of stars arranged in the form of a flattened disk or ring which circles countless solar systems." It goes on to say that our solar system is contained in one of this galaxy's spiral arms, approximately 30,000 light years from its center. The galaxy revolves around a mysterious center and also revolves on its axis, requiring approximately 200 million years making one complete revolution.

It is among this incomprehensible cluster of blazing stars, situated on the broad flat disk that circles through stellar space in cohesion with the Milky Way that is found the causal plane or what people refer to as Paradise. It revolves within the visible circle of resplendent suns and planets. The space between Earth and Paradise is composed of:

1. The entire astral plane
2. The lower mental realm

The sphere immediately surrounding and interpenetrating our Earth atoms is that which is called the astral; some refer to it as *Astralia*. So close is it in vibration to the Earth, it is a wonder more people are not more attuned to its presence. The atoms and essences of which it is constructed lie just beyond the range of the usual sense perception of Humans.

Indeed, many of the great philosophers have become intimately acquainted with this pervading unseen country. Plato says that men dwell, like frogs, in hollows and pools of "the lower valley" of our Earth, while the real surface of the Earth extends unseen into the region of ether above our atmosphere.

Plato and Socrates both refer to the etheric counterpart which extends beyond the solid periphery of Earth just as Human's etheric double extends beyond the physical form.

Our sun is surrounded by a sphere of radiating light composed of a solar fluid. This fluidic emanation is energized with the properties of all vitalic principles, magnetized in the pure, fiery soul of the Sun-laboratory. These solar rays flow outward from the Sun to fill the entire auric force field of our solar system. The Sun bathes every planet and its atmosphere with these electromagnetic essences.

In turn, from every planet and sun in our universe flow electromagnetic rivers, in and out, to and fro, ebbing and rising like great ceaseless tides which sweep on into the interstellar spaces.

As the perpetual flow of Human blood pulsates to and fro, in and out of a Human's arteries and veins, so do these positive-negative celestial rivers from geo-centers of planets and helio-centers of suns rise like streams of spiritual currents and circulate through the vast upper spheres of the cosmos.

The spirit worlds and the Human spirit form are composed of matter spiritualized; therefore, matter is spirit materialized. Action and reaction are always equal and correlative in the dynamics of the Universe. The auric waves emitted from the sun break into circling orbits or zones and each zone forms planes out of its own substance. The planes discard substances which become satellites.

When our solar system was in its infancy, our galaxy was one boundless, indefinable, unimaginable sea of liquid fire. As the undulating heat waves from the center, our sun, formed its zones and the escaping fiery comets formed planets, the system began to lose its heat. The measure of gravitation within the solar system equals the amount of heat lost by the sun. The mechanical motion of our planets, responding to the gravitational pull of the sun, is always the complement of heat exhausted from the sun.

The entire system came into existence through condensation. Our now solid planet once rolled through space in an attenuated, gaseous state. Our planet became solid through condensation as did the Human forms. The spirit of Humans now wear an outer crust of material substance, the Human physical form now wears an outer crust of material substance, our physical bodies, just as our once ethereal planet wears now a solidified crust on its outer sphere.

Ice becomes water, water becomes steam, steam becomes gas, gas becomes electronic particles, electricity becomes magnetism, magnetism becomes ether, ether becomes essence, and essence becomes spirit. Therefore matter is only the outer manifestation, or form, of an inner original force. All matter can be reduced to energy, which, instead of having gravitation, rises and escapes into space. If water or granite rock can be refined to steam or gas and caused to ascend into the atmosphere unseen, would not Humans possess the same quality? The inner original elements of all are always eternal.

Matter relates to the experience of the senses, which are limited to time and space. Spirit and spiritual faculties know neither time nor space. The senses can know only the realm of phenomena. Spirit knows only pure being. Inductive science can never unveil pure spirit. Only consciousness itself can suffice to complete the empirical process inward to the Cosmic Center of all manifestation. But science has already proved that external forms of matter are only outer appearances of ethereal, everlasting energies, which cannot be destroyed. Thus science knows that there exists Something which is eternal.

The World of matter is only condensed, materialized spirit; spirit wearing forms of minerals, plants, animals and Humans. Forms which, felt and touched, become real to the senses. But real what? Real phenomena. Not real eternally. Only Spirit is really real.

It is spirit that pervades space, breaking into waves and zones and circles of suns and planets, and vegetation and animals and Humans, all One Root Substance emanating from the Great Central Sun to express as form and ascending scales of consciousness. Since action and reaction are equal, it follows that if material worlds are spirit materialized, then the Spirit spheres must be body spiritualized. First must come the materializing or downward sweep into matter, followed by the ascending spiritualizing process. One complements the other.

The materialization of Spirit is attained by the translation of heat into mechanical gravitational motion of the heavens, while the spirit spheres are built by regaining the heat as it escapes from the forms created, especially from the Human form. And, as the particles escape, they also lose contact with phenomena to approach real reality. They escape the limits of gravity, time and space.

Science confirms that our material Worlds are created by condensation of vast solar rings. They must ultimately arrive at the conclusion that the material Worlds are losing heat, that condensation is escaping. But where? It reverses its original action. The inner essence escapes its bondage, its condensation, to form the unseen surrounding Spirit spheres.

Science concedes that the entire solar system was once filled with solar ether and that it was only a portion of a yet vaster distant stellar center. It recognized that the process of planetary formation was breaking off planetary bodies under the action of condensation.

The spiritual spheres are created by the reaction of this original action, a reverse action. Essences that "fall" into matter begin to disintegrate the material elements and escape toward the Great Central Sun that sent it forth, but in a higher state than when it fell.

The creation of the World of form and matter is through condensation of Spirit. Creation of the World of Spirit form and Spirit spheres is the dissolution of matter. Earth's solid form reflects, as in a mirror, the etheric and astral envelope lying all about it. The astral is the true "pattern World" of Earth. There is a continuous interplay of life and energy particles between the two Worlds, a never-ending round in the journey back and forth between the two terminals, gross matter and the refined etheric Otherworld.

THE CELESTIAL RIVERS IN SPACE

We know that our Earth is a gigantic magnetic battery. From its immeasurable mineral mountains beneath the sea, from its vast beds of iron, copper, zinc, gold, and tin raises an unceasing stream of electric currents into our atmosphere. It sweeps upward in a spiraling motion and is drawn toward the magnetic fields of Earth's North and South poles. These tremendous poles form atmospherically coiled receptacles of the multitudinous electrical currents from all parts of the planet.

The incessant stream of electric currents into these polar batteries results in self-illuminating vortices. These luminous lightings, evolved by the polar batteries, are called the *Aurora Borealis* for the northern lights and the *Aurora Astralia* for the southern. From these electrical lightings, electricity is transformed into a tenuous motive force of celestial magnetism. This magnetism rises like a warm vivifying vapor, even from the midst of mountains of ice and a continent of surrounding snow.

These incessant rivers of celestial magnetism float to encompass Earth's atmosphere, forming the basis of all atmospheric motion. It causes all electric variations, creates the formation of auroral vapor, the remarkable auroral and boreal splendors of the eastern sunrise and the western sunset, causes the floods of lights resulting from the sudden precipitation of cosmic atoms high above the Earth, and contributes toward the revolution of the Earth itself.

They form the magnetic force field of Earth, much as the vital forces generated in and by the nerve centers of the heart, brain and lungs sustain involuntary motions of the life force within Humans. These celestial emanations not only sustain the motion of Earth's life forces, but also sweep on into the upper regions to magnetize and vitalize the atoms of the astral spheres. These celestial rivers engirdle the Earth and are then drawn upward, principally at the north and south poles, until, freed from Earth's gravity, they flow into the rarefied ethers of heaven.

At the same time, there descends from the Sun the electromagnetic pranic forces which, entering the poles, are swept throughout Earth's magnetic field to vivify and activate new life forces on the Earth. These forces are especially active during the vernal and autumnal equinoxes.

From the South Pole of Earth there rises a magnetic stream, a river whose currents surge silently through interstellar space to pour into the zone near the Milky Way. From another point, a lighter river of force flows from the Milky Way to wend its way to the North Pole of our Earth, which is unchangeably electrical. It moves constantly and varies in strength from time to time. The stream flowing from Earth to these celestial regions is a positive stream. The one flowing into the North Pole is negative.

These celestial currents are like the flow of nerve fluid through the Heavens, the spiritual world, like a great throbbing heart, repelling one current and sending it earthward, and attracting another drawing it upward.

The spiritual spheres surrounding the planets, the spheres inhabited by those who once wore dense material forms, are bathed in rays of the spiritual counterpart of our blazing sun. These Rays penetrate the spheres with a luminous quality those of us on Earth find impossible to describe. There are no shadows there; no heat, no cold, no night, only a soft radiance that blends magically and mysteriously with the light of the body.

The streams and rivers and fountains of the Otherworld seem to glow with a self-luminescence, radiating their own immortal changes and transformations, but the plant kingdom never "dies." The firmament above breathes eternally the glory of the spiritual universe.

It is the fulfillment of Natural Law that the Earth World should supply certain atomic substances that help to create the surrounding Spiritual World. This does not mean that the material Earth creates the essences of which the Spiritual World is composed; these essences were created long ago by the Great Central Sun from which flows all created substances. But it does mean that after the spiritual essences have "incarnated" in matter, the planet resurrects and distributes substances that, obeying the higher Natural Laws, form themselves into an objective, organic World of spiritual reality surrounding the planet. The material planet is the womb where these essences become substances. In its evolutionary process, after the planet attains a certain evolutionary maturity, it becomes the spermatic foundation of the spiritual planes.

6.

First Communication With Edward in the Afterlife

Through the years, after I made conscious contact with the spiritual dimensions, I was able to speak with just about anyone I wanted to speak with. However, I had never had direct access to speak with Edward, the priest I had loved so deeply. This had always been frustrating for me. When I would ask about it, my soul would say that it was not being allowed, because my soul felt I would take his opinions as more valuable than my own and that I would still try to live by his values and desires more than my own.

In November of 2004, Twenty-five years after his death, the communication was finally allowed. I was allowed telepathic access to his consciousness. He began to speak with me as if the twenty-five years had not passed. I was furious; I felt justified anger. I was still angry with God for taking him when He did. It took weeks for me to work through the emotions of my loss, anger and grief all over again. I feel his presence occasionally now, when he is not busy doing something else. He is apparently very aware of me and what I am doing, but he doesn't interfere. Now I don't even choose to attempt to communicate with him daily as my communication with my own soul is the most important communication I have. He did remind me once, however, that the Master Jesus wanted to communicate through me. Jesus wanted His originally intentioned meaning of the Beatitudes corrected. I wrote down what He told me and printed out copies, two weeks after our communication resumed. At the time of his death, Edward and I were writing a book together about our relationship, but I never attempted to finish it. This book was written at a later time when communication was once again allowed by our souls again for a few weeks.

7.
Different Versions of the Afterlife

A friend and I were traveling by car from Boston to Sedona. We stopped to overnight in Oklahoma City. I called my friend Ann Smith. She mentioned that a mutual friend from California was back in town, because her mother was in critical condition in the Guthrie hospital. She said, "It is so wonderful and appropriate that you are here. Ramona was saying, just this afternoon, 'I wish we knew how to contact bj'." She gave us directions to the hospital and agreed to meet us there.

When my friend and I arrived at the hospital, we encountered Ramona's entire family. She was personally overwhelmed with relief to see us. "My mother will want to see you. If the nurses ask, you are a member of the family. Come with me." We entered the ICU. Her mother was awake, but hooked to many devices and hoses. Two other female members of the family were in the room. The patient's eyes seem to light up when she caught sight of me. I was relieved that she seemed to recognize me. I didn't really think she would remember me in her condition and since I had not seen her in almost ten years. I had read for her years before when she and her husband were going through a difficult period. She motioned weakly for me to approach the bed. I took her hand and placed a kiss on her forehead.

"I want to talk with you alone," she spoke weakly, but emphatically.

I turned to Ramona and shrugged my shoulders in question. She had heard her Mother's request. "Let's go girls. She wants to be alone with bj," she said as she ushered the other ladies from the room against their will. They had been told that their Mother had very few hours to live.

When we were alone, Mrs. Jones said, "Tell me what you know about the afterlife. Tell me what you know about heaven. I think you know."

"Well, I can tell you what my own Mother has told me. Maybe that will help. She says we get to create our own version of heaven. That once we get into the Light what we think is what we get. She says actually the same thing happens when we are on Earth, but that because of our training, and the influence of mass consciousness, that we do not realize we are creating our heaven or hell on Earth. She showed me a picture in a magazine recently of where she is." I described the picture to her. "She says the place is called Summerland and that in this place the 'weather' as we know it, is always warm and summery and that there are lots of fields of flowers there."

Mrs. Jones had a peaceful smile on her face. She thanked me, and God, for my coming through town at just the right time to get to visit with her. She asked me to pray for her to have an easy time getting out of her body, which I did. I visited with Ramona and my friend Ann. I left a number where I could be reached in Sedona. The next morning we left before sunup to continue our trip. When we arrived in Sedona, at our hotel there was a message from Ann. Ramona's Mom had left her body peacefully, during the night, with her family around her.

The next day in my meditation I saw Ramona's Mom on a white satin chaise lounge in the upper room of a lighthouse on a revolving platform. Around the stairwell of the lighthouse was filled with bookcases full of books, reachable from the spiral staircase. In the lower floor I perceived a kitchen and two people to cook, clean and deliver food to Mrs. Jones, whose responsibility was only to rest, read, to be waited on hand and foot and to eat from a box of Godiva chocolates on the table beside her. The 360-degree view allowed her views of the mountains and the ocean.

I called Ramona a week later, when she had returned to California, to give her my impression of her Mother's version of heaven. After I described what I had seen she reported that her Mom had always said that she fantasized about living in a tree house with nothing to do, but to read books, eat wonderful food and observe nature. Mrs. Jones never wanted to clean house or cook another meal. Ramona was relieved by the message that her Mom had indeed been able to fulfill her fantasy in heaven.

8.
Comments From Edward in the Afterlife

Edward was my fiancé who made his transition to the Afterlife in 1979, four days after I moved from Texas to marry him. He was an Episcopal priest and my soul was concerned that if I was allowed to communicate with him in the Afterlife I would still consider him my spiritual authority rather than attempting to communicate with my soul. Several years later the soul allowed me to communicate with him briefly. At that time we thought that we were to combine our efforts and to write about his experiences in the other dimensions. That did not happen. Now, he has been allowed to share with me what it is like where he is but only for this purpose.

Edward: Our love making that fourth night we were finally together gave me the energy to get out of my body. I do so regret having to leave you after such a short time of our finally getting to be together. I was so happy and more content than I had ever been in my life during that four days with you and your children. I'm glad I remembered to call you several times that day to tell you how happy I was, since that was our last day to be together on Earth.

    I see you have recently written and taught about the Bardo in your classes. I did have to go through the Bardo because I had so much grief to work through about leaving you and the priesthood and so much anger still toward the members of the Vestry who fired me. I had so much grief and felt I had been betrayed by so many people there at the church who had pretended to be my friends. Many days at the church I felt you were the only one on my side. The Vestry used the excuse that they felt I was no longer preaching from the Episcopal doctrine to let me go. At least that was the excuse they used. I now realize the events were created by us and our souls to get us both out of Lubbock and on to bigger missions.

I'm sorry you felt so betrayed by me after I convinced you to leave the security of your home and family in Lubbock. It did and does seem like such a harsh way to accomplish the soul's goal of getting us free to be who we really are. I did feel relieved when I found Bill Browning after I was over here and got permission from the soul to encourage him to help you with starting the greeting card business. Your artistic ability has continued to grow through the years and I am grateful you still make your lovely cards and share them with others. The energy you put in your paintings and cards blesses those who receive them.

I am so proud of you and all you have accomplished for yourself and our collective Oversoul. Your efforts have caused all of us in the Oversoul to grow wiser and stronger and to move into higher dimensions. What one aspect of the Oversoul does helps all the other members of the Oversoul.

I was helped by the counselors who work with those of us who are newcomers to this Otherworld to forgive those I felt had betrayed me and the grief I felt by having to abandon you after convincing you to give up your security in Texas.

It has been difficult because the Oversoul has not allowed us to be in communication. I felt so powerless to help you deal with so much grief you were experiencing being separated from your children, your friends, the church and everything you were used to in your life in Lubbock and your Mother's death at the same time. I was so angry and disappointed with the Bishops of Texas and Oklahoma and their treatment of you. Their attitude that you had killed me by making love with me and their judgment of our leaving our families to be together was painful to watch. Their telling you that you were no longer welcome to take communion was such a misuse of their power and an expression of their egos that I was even more disappointed in them and I had even more anger toward them.

I was stuck in the astral for awhile until I worked through the grief and anger. I've been allowed to attend many classes and to be present for many teachings from the Masters through the years, which has fulfilled my thirst for the truth and gained more awareness that much of what we were taught in seminary and teach from the *Bible* was not the truth. Ignorance of teaching untruths is forgiven here once we are exposed to what is truth.

I remember you enjoyed cooking and always brought delicious meals to the potlucks we had at the church. Newcomers here often eat and drink as we did on Earth. They still feel the need of food and drink. It takes a while to be aware that all we have to do is breathe the etheric substance from the air as nourishment. Believing we need to eat and drink was a hard habit for me to break and to accept that all we had to do was breathe. That which we do consume is discarded as vapors rather than waste matter from the body. Nourishment and life force are absorbed as we absorbed air and sunshine or light on the Earth plane. Here, the air itself holds an essence containing all the qualities necessary for the nutrition of these new forms. Cosmic Light emanating from higher planes pervades the lower planes and it is this cosmic substance that nourishes our spirit.

When we do choose to eat and drink, it is for fellowship and it is mostly the amazing fruits that grow here that we eat and the juice from the fruits that we drink. The fruits such as plums, cherries, grapes, grapefruit and melons grow without anyone needing to tend them. When they are picked, they are immediately replenished.

You will love the flowers here even more than the ones you grow and see on the Earth, my love. Their beauty and fragrance are amazing. Everything here is created mentally. When we have a need or we desire anything, we just hold a focus and intention on an image of the thing and that energy and focus cause the thing to appear. Creating things mentally or learning to manifest what we desire is something that we learn to do gradually. It is one of the first things we are taught in the Halls of Wisdom. It takes a while to become proficient at it. I've witnessed that this is one of the things you are teaching there to the people in your classes and I am grateful that you are helping them to be more advanced when they make their transitions to here.

bj: What kind of clothes do you wear and where do you get them?

Edward: Our clothes are also created by our thoughts. We can create clothes like what we wore on Earth in the beginning, but of course, since I hated wearing suits and ties that's not what I thought about. I was also through wearing black and a collar like when I was a priest so at first I created shorts and t-shirts since the climate here is warm and pleasant. I loved the freedom of not having to wear a "uniform." Now I have learned to create robes, not like the ones I wore as a priest, but these are more comfortable since we don't need to wear underwear. Sometimes I make them out of what we would think of on Earth as silk or even a lighter fabric that's available here but not on Earth.

Colors are way more varied here than what is available on Earth, since the light spectrum here creates colors not seen on Earth. Color and what the colors represent vibrationally are important and taught here. We are free to wear whatever we choose, but most folks choose full length flowing robes. The creative designs are limited only by the scope of our imagination.

Creating clothing or anything else requires a clear mental pattern and shape and a lot of mental focus to hold the vision of the desire to draw the energy and power to actually materialize it. In the higher dimensions, materials assume the appearance of silk, velvet, gold cloth, shining lace, or gauzy, gossamer veils, but I don't choose any of these adornments. The higher the plane the less the fabrics are like those on Earth; in the higher planes the fabrics become almost transparent with luminosity.

In the higher planes the clothing reflects the level and station of the spirit and some of the Masters wear jewels and symbolic colors of their station. Changes of clothing can be automatic according to one's thoughts or emotions or can be a matter of the will of the person according to their preferences. Clothing more or less reflects our inner character. On Earth we wore clothing to protect our physical bodies from the climate we were in. Here clothing is worn more as a symbol of the spiritual condition or station of the wearer.

Each plane contains its own vibrations; therefore, the clothing substance of one plane might be completely different from that of a higher plane. The substance is gathered by the will of the personality from the atmosphere, from the flowers, from other forms and magnetically treated until it evolves into the shape, beauty and perfection held in the mind of the one creating. This is taught in the schools.

In the planes of the Masters the clothing almost appears to be part of the being and they often wear crowns with jewels and jewel encrusted girdles around their waists and radiate energy from their crowns and ornaments.

In all things we are the creator of our own clothes, homes and surroundings here. We tend to gather and live near others who have similar interests and desires for learning. It is easy to recognize others who are similar in nature and thoughts by looking at their auras and the way they choose to dress. I tend to spend lots of time at the university and in the libraries when I'm not on duty in lower realms helping newcomers to adjust when they first leave their bodies and helping them locate their friends or members of their family who have come across before them. I've been allowed to travel to the astral to help, but only occasionally as I am still learning how to be of service without trying to influence or control others.

I've learned a great deal about controlling my thoughts and emotions since what we think here is obvious to others in a way that is much more apparent than it is on the physical plane, almost as if our thoughts and emotions are transparent to others. At first this is really unnerving to realize others are so aware of what one is thinking and feeling. But it is about our learning to control our minds and emotions. If we had been taught this while we were still on Earth there would have been less confusion in our communications, but our egos were so strong that we attempted to hide what we were truly thinking and feeling. Here we are more content and less judgmental.

The art of telepathy is not acquired without considerable effort. Once I reached Summerland, my communication with others became almost always telepathic. When I go into the astral to help others, I have to remember to actually speak aloud. Seldom, after being in Spirit for a while, do we feel the need to speak aloud unless it is for the purpose of singing or chanting.

Once I reached Summerland, I learned to think and communicate in the Universal Language. In these higher planes even though different languages are spoken, the consciousness perceives and understands what the others are communicating. There are no language barriers. We have learned to be clairsentient and use the language of the heart. Here communication is more from soul to soul.

I've moved though several dimensions during my stay here and feel most at home in Summerland. The beauty here is remarkable and not easily described since it is so far beyond what we were used to on Earth. The weather is always perfect and there are no irritating insects. The plants all vibrate with energy and the colors are exquisite. Being in the flower gardens is such a treat since the fragrances and the energy of flowers is so uplifting and rejuvenating.

The longer I am here the more I understand that everything is a part of the Oneness, a gift and a part of the Source of all creation. I do wish we had been more able to understand this while we were on Earth. Earth and all nature there is so beautiful, but I think we became immune to its beauty because we were so focused on just living and making a living and getting along that we forgot to appreciate what was free and around us as the beauty of nature. I wasted a lot of time in worry and being concerned about what other people were thinking of me and not enough in gratitude for all we were freely given by God to enjoy.

I still seek to learn more everyday and to help others as much as I can. Here we never stop seeking to know more truth and to practice what we are taught. We can never reach a point where there is nothing more to learn. For most of us, our desire for knowledge never ceases.

Some days my routine is to guide newcomers to the area that matches their spiritual level of understanding. Our first homes here are prepared for us before our arrival. They can only be constructed according to our thoughts and actions while we were on Earth. My home now is open to the beauty of nature here in Summerland and is almost like living without walls. The home and the objects are all beautiful and inspire me to be increasingly more creative. I had barely begun to paint before I left Texas and now I go to art classes and find great joy in painting, especially with watercolor just as you do. Here we all attempt to create more and more beauty.

Homes in Borderland are not nearly as beautiful as those here in Summerland, since our homes reflect the level of our spiritual understanding, our thoughts and actions. Sometimes I am asked to go to Borderland and help people there realize that only beneficial action for others can bring them real comfort and higher attainments. They eventually become aware that they must seek to help those who are vibrationally even lower than themselves. By helping others, a new Light and a new consciousness begins to awaken within them. It is rewarding to do this service since I remember what it was like for me when I was there.

When we were in Borderland, we had to unlearn much of what we believed to be truth when we were on Earth, especially spiritual truth. When I was in Borderland we attended classes where truths were clearly defined. People who remained bitter or who seemed content with their lot did not attend classes, so they remained in Borderland far longer. Fortunately for most, sooner or later an interest begins to stir within them and eventually they seek to move up to a higher vibration and more beauty. Some people require many incarnations before they make it out of Borderland.

Many Borderlanders still cling to the worn out theology taught on Earth. They hold fast to unprincipled and arbitrary rules they had been taught by the church leaders and remain stuck following those rules and thus remain in blind submission. They seem not to connect their theology of Earth with their present circumstances, and continue to be willing to bow down to the mediation of others, still allowing religious leaders who are still practicing and teaching old theology to stand between them and their God. I often feel regret for my part in being their intermediary when

I was in that position as a priest. Part of what got me fired from the church was teaching we can communicate with God without an intermediary and by not following the Book of Common Prayer.

Many people in Borderland still visit old confessionals, whispering to presiding priests, concerns about the lives they are now leading, complaining of their terrible oppressions and begging for prayers to help them out of their troubles. There are still some priests here who serve them and do so fully and sincerely believing they are following the course of truth since they also refuse to go to truth classes that would contradict what they were taught to believe on Earth. They still argue among themselves that their truth is the only truth.

Usually, when Borderlanders begin to realize that there are better realms of life, they send out a prayer for a loved one who has gone before them for help and seldom is such a call ignored. That is how many Borderlanders are brought to see the Light from higher Worlds by connecting with others who have gone before and have reached a higher understanding. They cannot go with the person who comes because the difference in vibration would be too painful. They have to start deliberately raising their own vibrations by serving those who are beneath them vibrationally, in order to move upward, but at least they then realize there are other planes that they can eventually attain.

Only by serving others are we able to eventually graduate into the higher realms. We of Summerland visit Borderland regularly to encourage and help Borderlanders in every way we are allowed, but the length of time we are there is not long because it feels so dense to us that we are grateful when we get to retreat back to Summerland.

In the higher Borderland, the atmosphere is more rarefied, the elements are more ethereal. In these higher Borderland levels, inhabitants constantly go to the lower regions to instruct others. They quickly learn that only through such services do they help themselves.

In the Midlands there are not only private homes but also many buildings I can only describe as apartments. Groups residing in the latter either prefer not to be isolated in private homes for personal reasons, or they reside together to carry out certain missions.

In the Midlands there are birds, flowers and many fruits. There are some beautiful homes and well organized grounds. There are lakes and mountains and schools of instruction, but not as many as in Highlands and Summerland.

On the planes of Highland there is considerably more Light. The homes are far more beautiful and the gardens and flowers radiate an unearthly beauty. Lakes are much larger and there are pleasure boats. Inhabitants there congregate to study the arts and there are colleges for various instructions very much like in Summerland.

There is beautiful music in Highland and Summerland. A great many inhabitants enjoy making musical instruments and playing them. I still play the piano and have a piano in my home in Summerland. There are mountains and streams and beautiful scenery in Highland and in Summerland.

On the planes of Highland, homes are symmetrical and artfully arranged, containing paintings, drawings and fine furniture. They walk as a means of getting around but some have also learned aerial flight. I've taken instruction in aerial flight, but as yet I have not mastered it.

In Summerland there are even more magnificent scenes and cities, rivers, extensive groves of amazing trees and lakes as clear as crystal. There are scientific institutions and laboratories. New inventions are created here and then impressed upon the minds of Earth inventors and researchers, but I spend more of my time in the arts, music and learning.

In Summerland, there are individual homes but many are arranged in groups. There are vast educational assembly halls, elegant meditation temples, colleges for astronomers, writers of poetry, books, music, and all artistic endeavors. Fountains of living water are everywhere and the flowers, as I have said, are beyond description.

In higher Summerland, where I visit occasionally, the scenes are almost beyond Human understanding. The homes there are mansions with extensive grounds and gardens. Flowers are more variegated and richly perfumed. There are arbors and vines and still more delicious fruits. Mountains are in the distance and the water in the lakes is transparent.

There are indescribable universities in these Summerland zones. Teachers from the celestial spheres are often here offering instruction. There are colleges relating to the Laws of Mesmerism, Electromagnetism. Intuitional and Inspirational influences are sent from Summerland to Earth, psychic and spiritual instructions are offered as well as meditation.

People from Summerland constantly descend to the lower realms to carry their messages of truth. It is from Summerland that most spiritual guardians of people on Earth are found. I am occasionally allowed, or better to say invited, to be a guide to someone on Earth.

There are many children who have crossed over that live in these higher vibrational areas. The children have guardians that live with them.

They also have teachers at the educational centers where they learn about nature, scientific principles, spiritual truth and controlling their minds and thoughts for manifestation. They also have amazing, fascinating, color-enhanced playgrounds built in such magnificent forms to expose them to geometry and mathematical principles. As the children achieve more and more understanding of these principles, the colors of the equipment change to indicate their progress and they graduate to new, and more complex levels of educational playgrounds. Other outdoor areas are available for scientific experiments to demonstrate Natural Laws such as gravity, photosynthesis, propulsion and more.

In Summerland there is only beauty. There are no insects other than butterflies and dragonflies. There are no beasts, only the animal pets Humans loved on Earth who join their Human once they have crossed over.

The joy of living here is beyond description. Poets have attempted to describe it, artists have tried to catch visions on paper and canvas. The very atmosphere here is mellow and glowing; everything seems to be breathing with a living force, even the greenery. There is never an upset, never violence. All here is tranquil and peaceful. Even the clothing here appears to shine.

In Summerland, people are busy pursuing truth. We understand the Law that regulates our society and we harmonize with it. We understand the purpose of the soul is perpetual spiritual growth.

Everything in Summerland moves in perfect harmony. Over here we not only reap the good of what we have sown, we also experience the happiness we wished for but which we never seemed to master while we were on Earth. Again, I tell you that the four days I was allowed to spend with you were the happiest of my life there.

Some of the fountains here flow with what we call living waters. These are highly energized waters channeled from the lakes and rivers of the higher planes. There are some on the lower planes also, but those are fountains whose waters have medicinal properties that rejuvenate and regenerate.

A rainbow arch of transcendent splendor is suspended over higher Summerland and its radiating colors seem to weave circle within circle, forming an aura over the entire area. The Living Waters of the beautiful fountains are often raised to great heights, refracting many changing colors, and spraying a shower of silver droplet in all directions. Flowing with and through the waters are strains of celestial music.

Near where I live there is a central building shaped like a gigantic pyramid. It is pure white. It is seven stories high. The main floor is almost a city within itself. This is the grand social room where people gather for companionship and pleasure much as do people on Earth gather at their country clubs. The ground floor may be opened to reveal one huge pavilion, or it can be portioned to provide smaller rooms for various activities like some of the large conference centers on Earth.

On some occasions when the entire room is opened, there is dancing much like a festive garden party on Earth. There is music for dancing, both inside and out in the open gardens among the beautiful flowers similar to what you saw at Versailles when you were in France. Two of the walls are not enclosed. They are composed of archways covered with colorful flowering vines and evergreens. The room is furnished with sofas, chairs and tables, beautifully formed and exquisitely carved, again very much like you saw in Versailles.

The second floor is devoted to musical and dramatic presentations. Here we gather for symphonies, concerts, operas, dramas, vocal and instrumental soloists, ballet and even motion pictures which are multi dimensional.

The third floor is an art gallery displaying a most incredible collection more amazing than what you saw at the Louvre. There are reproductions of great masterpieces created on Earth, but not the reproductions of the crucifixion and the bloody war murals you witnessed in the Louvre.

The fourth floor is a museum of sculpture. Here also we see statues of prominent people, mostly Humans who became important through earthly fame; many are of great philosophers, musicians, statesmen, artists and initiates. The great hall itself is a work of art, covered with gold leaf and flowers, crystals and precious gemstones. The entire hall is a museum of spiritual antiquities.

On the fifth floor is a library. There are other libraries about Summerland, but this is the most extensive. This one contains treasures seldom found on Earth. These are the manuscripts written by Masters and initiates. A few of these priceless manuscripts may still be found on Earth, but most are hidden. Most have long since been completely destroyed by Humans. Here, there are fresh, clean copies as if they were only recently written. This is one of my most favorite places to spend time studying the works of the Masters.

The sixth floor is devoted to special classrooms for teaching meditation, psychic development and spiritual illumination. Here teachers gather to instruct those who are interested in developing God-realization.

This is a very busy floor since many people of Summerland are interested in such an achievement.

The seventh floor, the capstone of the pyramid, is the most important of all the great rooms. This is the sacred hall of worship. Lectures are offered here conducted by the Masters from upper planes that are qualified to teach.

This is the smallest of the great halls. Seating is arranged as an amphitheater, succeeding rows above and behind each other. Many hundreds of people can be here at the same time. The seats in no way resemble uncomfortable stadium seats. They are more like cushioned lounge chairs, joined together, yet structured so that they collapse in order to be put away when more room is needed. Here we express our prayers, our aspirations and our profound gratitude to God, the Giver of All Life.

Etheria includes Borderland, Highland, Summerland and Paradise and it is just as natural a World as is the solid World where you live. It has its laws and we can view the stars. We have everything you have because everything on Earth that is not reabsorbed by the Earth ascends to become a physical part of Etheria.

This is such a wonderful World; there is little to behold but happiness. Even witnessing the trials and tribulations, like what you have been going through, does not necessarily bring us worry and unhappiness, because we can see the causes behind such actions and often can see the end of them. That is, we can see that the problem is going to end well, or we can see where the suffering involved was brought about by one's own thinking or carelessness. We are not allowed to interfere with Freewill, but can do our part to limit the suffering if our help is sought.

In observing a Human I know and care for who is experiencing sorrow, I feel sorrow to some degree, but not for myself. I feel it as compassion for someone else. I think it must be awareness that all things are happening as they should at all times; that makes a Human able to overcome their emotions and not be ruled by them.

bj: Why have you stayed out of a physical body for so long? It seems to me a long time to stay in the spiritual dimensions?

Edward: I have a mission here just like I did on Earth. Here I spend time welcoming and helping people who have just crossed over to adjust to their astral body and to help them find whatever help they need to begin to adjust. Many who cross over find it very difficult to believe they are dead. I work toward teaching them that they are not the body they left behind but that they are a unit of consciousness that never dies. I stay very busy every day, but I also let myself have time to just appreciate the beauty of where I am and I continue to be both teacher and student here.

I know you wanted to have me walk-in to another's body so we could be together again as a couple, but that was not and is not the will of the Oversoul. You work best alone, which is not a judgment but an observation on my part and the opinion of our Oversoul. You are so independent and determined to accomplish your mission, there is really no time for you to have a romantic relationship in your life at this time. You still have much to accomplish, so much to get out into the World from the wealth of information you have obtained from the Masters in the last forty years. I am relieved to see others reaching out to assist you to get the books you've written and especially the 49 Rays of God information out and available.

Several others have helped financially and by editing what you have brought through from this side of the veil and of course Judi's and Ann's help in obtaining a home for you and a home for Namaste Enrichment Center. I regret that I did not make sure you had a home before I left. Cindy and Farris created and offered a place to make your books available and a format for you to offer what you've learned to their group. This is indispensable to our Oversoul and your work with the Hierarchy.

As I said, I have not mastered aerial flight as yet, but we have other conveyances here; one is like a flying carpet. I have not as yet traveled to other planets in person, but I currently attend classes to improve my clairvoyant vision to begin to see the other planets and what takes place there. I know you are much more knowledgeable about other civilizations and planets than I am since you came back to Earth from another civilization beyond this solar system.

Hopefully, the Oversoul will allow us to continue our discussion in the future. I have so enjoyed getting to visit with you like this and to share some of what goes on here. I intend to remain in Summerland unless our Oversoul points out that I could be of more service elsewhere. Adonai, Dear One. Be well. Be happy. Your Edward.

9.
Edward's Experiences in Summerland

No one enters the realm of Summerland until they have attained the spiritual consciousness to experience at-one-ment with the conditions of light, joy and peace. There are a million imperceptible gradations between heaven and hell and between Borderland and Summerland. People in the Lowlands remain there of their own choice. They often visit the Highlands, attempting to live there, but they cannot breathe comfortably nor do they feel at ease in the higher light. They return to a level that corresponds to their own inner vibration. There, they attend classes and perform services for others until their inner growth makes it possible for them to be comfortable moving to a higher plane.

Borderland and Summerland have a million crisscrossing paths, with homes, valleys and cities in between. The only law binding one to any particular level is their level of fitness or readiness. When a Lowlander, through the development of their own inner light, can dwell comfortably in a more elevated atmosphere there is no one to forbid their movement upward. No one can enact a law concerning their inner growth. It is a matter of personal attainment.

Hell, purgatory, Lowlands, Highlands, Summerland and Paradise are not specifically divided. A person notices they have left a certain level of vibration, or city only by awareness of their own personal discomfort. A Lowlander will only become aware when they begin to have trouble breathing in the rarer ethers of the next vibrational gradation. There are no physical signs indicating borders between dimensions.

Each soul is measured by their soul limits, not their city limits. When souls do reach a new level of understanding and service, they are welcomed into the higher frequency levels with celebrations. They do not leave their friends, no love ties are severed, and they experience no grief or sorrow as they might feel on Earth. A bond of deep affection enables those who ascend to guide those left behind and to assist them on their own ascent when they are ready. A Master from higher planes arrives at the celebration and delivers a lecture telepathically and those who have prepared through study and practice perceive the message.

Classes are available in all levels for psychic or spiritual training just like on Earth. As you have experienced, some folks seek to know more and are willing to practice what they are taught and some don't. Training in clairvoyance, clairaudience, clairsentience, psychometry, trance states and visionary perception are taught everywhere here. Those living in Borderland are usually less interested in such study and practice. They are generally content to live just as they did on Earth. Many continue to live uneventful lives, doing little harm and little good and they exist that way until they are allowed to incarnate again for another experience on Earth or one of the other planets.

Those of us who have made it into higher planes realize that there are still higher potentials and some develop the higher potentials and move on up. I personally am content to remain in Summerland. There are still levels of Summerland above where I currently live and I shall work toward moving there, but I feel my current gifts best serve working with newcomers to the spirit world. I can visit higher planes periodically, but the visits are of a short duration because, as I have stated, one has to match each area vibrationally to be comfortable

When the Masters come here to teach, they put a veil over their radiance so we can observe them, but we do not see their individual expressions because of the veil. We do, however, perceive their intent and expressions vibrationally as you did when the Master visited you to create the Namaste organization and later to convince you to write His version of the Beatitudes.

In my work with newcomers, I observe that many who believe in a more orthodox religion are surprised that they are not met by an Angel ready to place a harp in their hands and led to a choir where they will forever play harps and sing praises to God.

As with hell, heaven is many things to many people. Even the degenerates who descend first to hell, eventually experience glimpses of higher realities. A person who has crossed over can only perceive their surroundings and the possibilities only to the degree that they have created an awareness of perfection in their own being while they were incarnated on Earth.

Very few people descend immediately into the darkest depths of hell and a very few ascend directly into Paradise. Most linger a while in Borderland, a longer time in Highland, and a much longer time in Summerland. Some either then reincarnate or some eventually reach the pure causal regions of what one would think of as the real heaven.

Since Summerland is a realm of the mental plane, it is the heaven most people live in the longest; it is this plane that most people refer to when they speak of heaven in general. Summerland is the world in which thought force molds life force. That which we think on becomes what we think just like it does on Earth. The only difference is here we are aware of that Law, but not so much is it apparent when we are in our Human form. Life would certainly be easier for Humans if they knew and practiced that Law of thoughts become things.

Summerland is as natural to those of us living here as it is living on Earth for Humans. The Law of Cause and Effect is more instantaneous here so it is more easily perceived.

Beauty is everywhere here. Flowers here are not seasonal. There are many that do not appear on Earth. I have witnessed you painting flowers that do not appear on Earth and you saying, when people ask what flower is that, you respond it is an Atlantian flower, which always amuses me. The petals of the flowers here glow with light, some soft, others flashing. The flowers almost seem to be jewels. Petals of the lilies resemble pure pearl. Leaves of foliage glisten and sparkle as if they are covered with tiny crystals and diamonds. As they sway in the breeze, the air carries soft low tones of music into the atmosphere.

Over each city or region hangs a mist, bathing everything with radiance. Over one, the luminescence might be pink and over another it might be blue, but I know the one you would love most is a soft violet. Each color has a meaning and purpose, just like all the Rays of God. In this case, the activity and spiritual level of its inhabitants affects the color of the luminescence. There are colors here that the Human eye cannot as yet perceive on Earth.

Each home here has its own terraces and gardens. Where earthly homes are constructed of wood, brick and stucco, homes here seem to be of coral, marble, alabaster and jasper, and sometimes sapphires, rubies, emeralds, pearls and amethysts are added. Every home gleams. There is nothing coarse about the materials the homes are made from and there are no storm windows or tinted windows that mar the beauty of open areas because the Earth's sun never glares here. The light is constant here as opposed to the sun rising and setting where you are. The rays here are made of diffused, ethereal light and warmth that doesn't cause shadows.

The actual buildings are erected by loved ones or friends who have previously entered Summerland so when the new arrival comes their home is ready. Homes here are usually set among trees, gardens and woodlands. Often they are constructed by souls who were architects, masons and builders on Earth and who follow the same occupation in Summerland, but who no longer build with hammer, saw and nails. In training classes they learn how to "raise up" a structure mentally, molding the ethers of their walls and domes into solid substance and look much like homes on Earth, before they take on the colors and vibrations of the occupants.

Building is not only a chosen occupation of many; it is also the service of pleasure. No one works for pay, but rather for the joy of working, serving and the spiritual reward. Others serve in other fields. I enjoy creating gardens more than buildings. I appreciate there is no dust, decay, storms or rain here.

Some buildings here are elaborately ornate. Some are unfurnished, unembellished awaiting newcomers. Usually there are no doors to close out the beautiful views; only soft translucent, flowing, gauzy draperies that light can penetrate. Pictures on the walls often reflect the record of a person's Earthly accomplishments.

There are carvings, sculptures and fountains unlike anything on Earth. Things here are always beautiful and there is always a feeling of peacefulness and serenity. Here, there is no time so there is a sense of quiet contentment.

People who have experienced either a lingering or exhausting illness are taken to what are called Havens of Rest as soon as their silver cord is severed. Some are aware there are loving people attending them; some are in a state of deep sleep. I've noticed you mention these Havens of Rest in your classes and that you perceive the newcomer to be wrapped in a pink energy that reminds you of cotton candy until their etheric bodies are healed. While they are in this sleeping state, words of wisdom and comfort are whispered to them to reach their minds and hearts before they awaken so to shield the soul from more unnecessary shock.

The Havens of Rest are softly tinted buildings usually set on the crest of a hill overlooking valleys of grass, flowers and woodlands. Each room is open to an amazing view. The sleeping person's body is treated with a down pouring of colored lights from the Rays of God to speed their healing. In the gardens, some loved ones and friends wait, not like in a hospital waiting room because nothing here is that bleak, but they wait in the gardens until the first sign of consciousness awakens in the newcomer. This is why some people report seeing friends and family members when they first enter the spirit world.

Husbands and wives, parents and children, sisters and brothers and friends all meet again after the interval of their parting. They meet here and become aware that they sometimes were also approached while they slept by these departed souls while they were on Earth.

The family reunites but considering the various temperaments, spiritual development and personal tastes, they will seldom share a home on this side. They can unite without becoming a family as they were on Earth. When it becomes clear that each soul will live upon the spiritual level that fits with their spiritual development, there is no sorrow when loved ones move into different houses. Here serenity is more important so often individuals develop individual opinions, tastes, dispositions, habits and culture that would make living together in one house difficult as it is on Earth. Therefore, often a family may establish a compound with the homes of various family members encircling a common area.

Every soul that arrives in Etheria has, during their lifetime on Earth, become conditioned to societal limitations; however, in the Afterlife, we can all choose the circumstances of where we live. On Earth, blood relationships establish families. In heaven, a higher law is followed. Family relationships are lifted into spiritual bonds. Souls drawn together by the Law of Spiritual Attraction create spiritual friendships and companions. Pure affection, whether between members of a family or not, is an attribute of the spirit. Associations we had on Earth only continue here if the relationship is harmonious. The Law of Attraction governs all relationships here.

bj: That's a relief. I can't imagine not being allowed to live alone and being required to live with my family. I would have great difficulty being serene.

It is more usual here for folks to group together because of shared interests in spiritual growth, art, music or any other interest rather than to remain in one dwelling with people just because they were our family on Earth. Personalities learn to tolerate separateness and solitude differently than their egos do on Earth.

Music enters into so many phases of life over here. Music and blended colors are important, but different than on Earth. Here, love seems to radiate from the music itself. The subdued tones of the music affect every environment here, the changing hues and tints of clothing, the buildings and landscapes. Flowers and foliage take on deeper and more radiant colors when musical tones are played nearby and even the water sings here.

Music has a strange power here. Through music we are taught to comprehend certain ideas. It is as if we are being told things through the music. There does not seem to be an actual voice, but the mind interprets certain teachings through music in a way that is subliminal. Part of each of us in connected to the Universal Mind of God or the Source. Listening to the celestial music makes connection to the Universal Mind easier because of the vibratory waves connected to it.

Through music we seem to receive teachings, which are hidden in the files of our subconscious. Ideas seem to ride on the musical waves and enter conscious awareness easier than speech. Here, though no individual voice speaks, it is as if we are in touch with the Mind of God or Universal Mind through the inspiration of music.

When I first arrived, I continued to use language as it is spoken on Earth. Slowly, as time passed, I found myself thinking in terms of musical refrains. Being constantly surrounded by the language of music, my mind began to express itself in a strange new language related to symphonies, melodies, songs, hymns, anthems and chants. I know you think of yourself as musically illiterate and think of it as noise, but I think you will find this music more to your liking. I've heard you tell people that Earth music is not as harmonic as the music you were used to on Venus and Earth music just sounds like noise to you.

I don't have a way to describe the language of music as it is employed here, to disclose an understanding of a higher language as well as the scientific truths. But music itself unfolds glorious lessons in celestial principles, including the principles of communication. Unbelievably wondrous music fills the whole of Etheria, each of its zones synchronizing with the majestic rhythm of the universe.

There are Universities of Music and conservatories where I study music. These buildings are devoted to the creation of music and the manufacture of musical instruments. We are involved not only in the study of music, but its combinations and effects as musical sounds in other ways. Some are devoted to dispensing musical inspiration to people on Earth who are talented in composition; others in playing, others in singing. Some concentrate on concert music, some ecclesiastical, some popular and some operatic. People on Earth are carefully selected and, during hours of sleep, are similarly trained as receptive vehicles for inspiration. A chain of invisible workers from the colleges in Etheria go to the churches, opera houses and concert halls to inspire.

Music enters almost all facets of life on the inner planes. Everything seems to have its birth in the vibrational essence of musical tones so that everything seems ultimately to have been created through music, music and blended colors, and the energies of love.

Different renditions of music create "thought forms," or accumulations of vibratory essences into patterns, which reflect the inner feelings of the artist or group of artists. The beauty of the music must first come from the composer and then from the artists who interpret the composition. The composer needs to not only be acquainted with the technicalities of the profession but also with the thought forms that it will induce.

Fountains here often emit jets of water, each releasing simultaneously a note of music. The blending of all the notes creates indescribable melodies, much as an organ with many stops. Earth's music is but a faint echo of heaven's music. Humans receive occasional snatches of incomparable harmony as they come through to Earth. But it is dulled and muffled, like sounds penetrating a fog.

bj: Since I was allowed to speak with you again, I've continuously heard faint and distant, what I would describe as "circular" music in my head. It sounds like it is made by someone playing bagpipes. Does that make any sense to you? It's not too irritating or distracting, just constantly there. The description you just gave of it being muffled and sounding like it is penetrating a fog is a better description.

Edward: It is possible you are hearing the sounds of the swirling colors here. They sometimes sound like that to me but it is more likely that what you are hearing, my love, is a frequency being sent from here to make it possible for you to capture the thoughts I am sending you.

We are taught in the Afterlife that sound has healing qualities for the new arrivals. Those who have endured a long, debilitating illness, or who arrive through sudden accident or violence and have experienced a degree of shock, are taken to a Rehabilitation Center. There, instead of being given medicine, they are surrounded by music, which is carefully selected by the doctors for the patient. These are different than the Havens of Rest centers.

Most Humans are not yet aware of the extent to which the physical body reacts to the sound of sympathetic music. The rhythm of melodies possesses curative properties. Occasionally the music is completely eliminated and the soul is immersed in what we call the Great Silence.

bj: I prefer the silence.

Edward: Yes, I've noticed you not only prefer solitude but also silence and don't play the radio or television. If we had ever gotten to live together that might have become a challenge for us since I am so musically inclined.

bj: How do you see me and my surroundings?

Edward: Everything on Earth emits an aura, and as spirits we discern physical objects by means of the aura surrounding them. So I see your aura and the aura of your home, which are lovely and peaceful.

bj: Do you have a governmental organization there?

Edward: On Earth there are divisions like counties or parishes and states. We have similar divisions here. There is a Center of Inquiries in each county here. One might call it a Bureau of Vital Statistics in that it houses complete information concerning everyone in the county.

Each bureau is under the supervision of very highly spiritualized people who have been in the Afterlife a long time. They do not belong to Summerland but they return periodically to carry out jobs appointed to them. This is a tremendous job.

The files from the Bureau of Statistics are not like those of Earth. It is as if we have motion pictures of everyone's lives. The managers of these bureaus know the problems of the newly arrived for instance, and what are apt to be temptations and possible mistakes. They are aware of the grief experienced and the need to return to Earth to visit loved ones, so this type of guide is necessary for any particular problem.

I had to get a special dispensation in our situation for me to get intervention from Bill Browning to help you to deal with your grief and help you financially and physically to create the greeting card company once you started painting. I could not "make" anyone help you, but I was able to let Bill feel my grief and the powerlessness I felt at not being there to help you. I sent him images of you in his sleep so that when he did meet you at the seminar, he recognized that he had a responsibility to help you in my place since I was not able to help physically from here.

I, of course, wanted to help you myself, but the counselor I spoke with knew this was not correct protocol, so she arranged the possible connections for you to reconnect with the Rainbow Bread man at Albertson's and she let me merge with Bill Browning emotionally to inspire him to help you.

These officials are really kind counselors, ready to advise newcomers concerning the first steps in a strange new world, as well as helping others decide on occupations and activities most spiritually advantageous to their growth. They also advise the inhabitant when a loved one is arriving from Earth, if it is not already known, so that the Human may be properly met.

Such supervision really isn't government. It is more like a counseling bureau. Each bureau is under the guidance of one still higher. For instance, our bureau may receive instructions from a higher plane that a certain mission is to be performed on Earth. Then our bureau members select those best qualified to perform the mission. Those on higher planes are involved in principles, while those on our planes are involved in the personal.

Government here is by natural Law. Natural Laws do not need enforcing. These Laws are easily perceived in Etheria and are not easily discerned by Humans. Some people on Earth are becoming increasingly aware that their thought forms affect their daily lives.

Those who live in the higher vibrations of Etheria need no discipline, no laws, no organization, and no government to keep them in order. Being nearer the seat of Divine Law, they have perfect understanding of each principle. Each descending area sees increasing imperfection as persons tend to evade the Divine Principles. They think more of themselves than of service to others.

Regarding actual governing bodies, there is only one God of the universe, but there are Solar Gods applying their efforts to solar systems; there are Planetary Gods occupied with each planet; and even Master Souls in charge of cities in the higher vibrational areas.

Such Masters could be called governors, or a ruler, but not as Earth knows them. Rather they are guides, teachers and counselors. A Master or Ruler is usually many thousands of years old in spirit. Each is equipped with patience, kindness, knowledge of Human sympathy, and all the highest spiritual attributes. They possess knowledge of the desires and needs of all in their domain. They make sure that the Divine Principles operate consistently.

Above all is the Great Cosmic Christ and over Him the Creator of all universes. Each sphere, each city is peopled by souls of like mind living in harmony together. This does not mean I have no freedom of choice. I could choose to do wrong, but I know better. If I were to do wrong I would no longer be allowed to remain in Summerland. Also my counselor would advise me before I could make such an error. I recognize the Laws here and I live by them. These Laws do not deny freedom of choice, but living within the Laws is what creates a feeling of happiness.

Each city has a leading magistrate and their home is near the central building in the hub of the city. All roadways lead toward that residence. All major decisions proceed from the magistrate. Under the magistrate, vast staffs of dedicated workers appointed by the magistrate carry out the various duties. Most of these workers are souls who could long ago have departed for higher realms but who have chosen to remain where they are because of their love of service.

Since the cities are composed mostly of universities and centers of learning, each center has its own Headmaster, and separate departments, much as Earth's colleges. The teachers often remain for years and years guiding hordes of souls through their training. If they decide to leave for higher realms, others equally dedicated replace them. Such service carries its own reward. Some spend time teaching and training in one area while living in another.

Teaching is the most prominent occupation here, but there are many others. People who were performing occupations on Earth that are not needed here, may choose other occupations. Everyone here does something to add to the beauty and harmony of their area. The system for living to work that enslaves many Humans is not required here so other ways to add service are developed.

A person who has always desired to travel can go to the ends of both this world and the Earth. Most people choose to mind travel, but some prefer to actually travel in their astral body to different locations. When they have fulfilled their desire to travel they turn their attention to whatever means of service they feel they would enjoy.

Mind power is essential in all occupations, and it becomes a challenge to keep trying to outdo one's previous efforts. In Etheria occupations become more like a challenging game to improve one's own efforts. Training is available to anyone seeking to learn a new vocation. I am aware you wrote and have taught Life Is a Spiritual Game – These are the Rules with information given to you by our Oversoul. These students who have taken your classes will be more prepared to face life after death than those who have ignored this information.

I remember counseling many men who floundered after retirement and felt a loss of identity and purpose. Retirees, especially men, find the Afterlife and these regions too peaceful and not to their liking. They miss the challenges, competition and solving problems. They often desire to return quickly to Earth life. These souls reincarnate quickly not because they have to but because they want to. They are at a loss to know how to help others spiritually. They find the path to spiritual progression empty of any appeal. On Earth they had much, and they long to possess things of Earth again. They desire to be where their shallowness can be covered with Earth's prosperity, where their inner darkness can be lighted by their accomplishments.

The cleverness and guile that gained them prosperity and attention on Earth is of no credit in spirit. Here it is not one's brain power, but their character that establishes the quality of their life. A clever mind does not help to create or build a spiritual body. That is accomplished only by the amount of love ingrained in the character, not the degree of knowledge one possesses, unless it be knowledge based on love, or love based on knowledge.

May you be well, my love, I know this is a challenging time for you and many others going through such an unprecedented event. You are making good use of your quarantined time to write and teach this spiritual information and painting and sending more of your lovely cards. May you be richly rewarded for your dedication and service.

Adonai,
Your Edward

10.
Edward's Comments on Religion and Prayer on Earth and in the Afterlife

Edward: It is interesting that you have asked me about religion here in Etheria since you know me well enough to know it would be one of the first things I checked out after I finished with balancing my karma, had my life review and made it through the Bardo. I spent years of my life studying World religions and then went through seminary to become a priest, because I was searching for the truth about God and Humans. I never felt completely comfortable teaching the Bible after I became aware of how many times it has been retranslated, rewritten and re-edited. But, once I agreed to be an Episcopal priest, I had to commit to teaching from the directions in the Book of Common Prayer and the scriptures recommended for each day and week.

I was compelled by the rules of the diocese doctrine to follow the Book of Common Prayer. The dogma of the Episcopal Church was less offensive to me than that of many other domination choices and was less regulated. I went along, so to speak, for years doing what was expected until about 1978 when things started bothering me more about what I was being expected to teach and the rituals and routines I was expected to follow. I began to have discomfort presenting myself as a supposed authority not only about the Bible, but about religion in general. I started feeling like we were missing the point and that the real point was about spirit and, what seemed like in the church, a lack of personal awareness of spirit. It is not even easy for me to attempt to explain the discomfort, but it was as if I was representing something that wasn't true.

I had begun to meditate in private, of course, and started feeling that I was receiving inspiration, thoughts, messages, suggestions; not sure what to call it. The suggestions seemed to be for me to leave the priesthood so when the vestry became uncomfortable with things I started to express, I felt I should leave Saint Christopher's, leave the priesthood and return to geology, which is what I was trained to do before I became a priest.

As I readied to leave Lubbock and Saint Christopher's, I became increasingly aware of how much I would miss you. I knew my marriage to Martha was ending. She never liked being a priest's wife. She had begun to drink daily and I knew it would be a relief to separate not only from the church and the priesthood, but also the marriage.

After your Mother's death, when I began to communicate from Oklahoma with you, the messages I received in meditation became more repetitive that I should encourage you to join me. I know it was unfair of me to pressure you to give up your security there and to come with me without offering you security and marriage, so I filed for the divorce.

The changes we both had to go through and the choices our changes forced on others was difficult for both of us, but I felt we were both being compelled to change and to be together. I was so relieved when you finally agreed to come be with me. I was given no inkling from my soul that I was going to leave you so soon. I'm sure if the soul had let me know, the guilt would have stopped me from convincing you to come. That was not what needed to happen for you to be free to live out the future your soul had in mind.

The circumstances of your excommunication by the Bishops of the Episcopal Church also had to be in God's plan so that you, too, would be lost enough to seek direct connection with your soul. But, my love, I can't imagine how difficult it all was for you to be abandoned by me and the church and to give up your children to be raised by their father in Texas. You survived and you have become an example to so many others to be brave, to risk and to follow suggestions from their souls. It is important for people to understand that the soul only gives suggestions, not orders, and the Law of Free Will is never rescinded.

Now to attempt to answer your question about religion here; crossing over to the spiritual dimension does not immediately imbue one with the truth. People bring their religious beliefs with them. Many expect to "meet God" or to, at least, be met by Saint Peter or their savior Jesus. They also expect to be judged by God. They are confused and bewildered when they learn they will be their own judge.

In the beginning, those who retain their old theology and dogmas usually find others who are still operating from those rules and beliefs and they hang out together. There are church buildings here and they gather there to follow services that are familiar to them. Denominations of Christians separate into various groups just as people on Earth divide themselves into those who believe in the second coming of Jesus, those who believe in Judgment Day, those who believe in hell and judgment.

Religious convictions held during Earth life determines where a person will first go after they have made it through their Bardo experience. Jews, Catholics, Fundamentalist Christians, Moslems — all who continue to hold fast to their beliefs and rituals — tend to stay together with others of their similar beliefs.

Souls frequently come and go through many lives as members of the same race and religious beliefs. They refuse to change their religious beliefs and this draws them into another incarnation almost duplicating a previous one.

Many Catholics, as well as Protestant fundamentalists, often hold the same views they did before death. They come here believing they will sleep until some distant ay and when they awaken they are convinced they have been asleep for years and are confused that they are still in the same place as when they crossed over. There are many counselors who attempt to help these souls to understand the truth, but many are so conditioned that they do not believe anything that conflicts with what they had been taught on Earth.

Each denomination holds to its own theological beliefs. The Baptists and Mormons baptize, the Methodists sprinkle, and Catholics sprinkle Holy Water to clear the sins of babies. The Moslems pray five times daily, the Buddhists lay fruits and gifts at the feet of the Buddha statues.

Religious fanatics are not easily convinced that the 'end of the World' was the end of their life span on Earth. Once the counselors or teachers introduce them to Spiritual Laws by showing them evidence of how the Laws work, their minds are sometimes changed and they can move toward a belief in a greater God than the one they were taught about on Earth.

It is not uncommon to find whole communities still practicing their old religion of Earth, even with its bigotries and prejudices. They engage in the same rituals and formal ceremonies in churches erected for this precise purpose. They are allowed to follow their own beliefs and to delay their own progress. They are exposed to visitors from higher realms who seek to enlighten them, but often their beliefs are so strong that they refuse any change and no pressure is applied to get them to change.

The creeds and dogmas of Earth are carried over into Etheria. These faithful remain determined to follow their beliefs until they have a spiritual awakening. As a few move upward to higher vibrations, more newcomers arrive with their limited Earth beliefs. Those who, while on Earth, studied mysticism, spiritual truth, psychic development and Spiritual Laws move into higher planes quickly.

More and more people on Earth seem to be moving away from traditional religion and are no longer willing to allow others to tell them what to believe. They are rejecting the dogmas of discipline. Some are now seeking personal contact with God or at least with their own souls. There seems to be a spiritual revolution happening on Earth, which is encouraging. So many more books, programs and teachers are available now, like you, who are teaching Spiritual Laws, meditation and soul communication than there were back in the 1970's.

Throughout Etheria, there are great temples for worship of the One God. Many of the teachers who come to Highland and Summerland come from higher realms and encourage the unfoldment of individual psychic and spiritual gifts. There is no chance in Etheria for practicing psychic fraud as there is on Earth, because fraud is quickly revealed by a person's aura.

Etherians attend worship services on Earth, especially at Christmas and Easter, to increase the energy of these services in order to increase the possibility of those attending to open more to higher vibrations and truth.

bj: What about the *Bible*? I tried to understand it and studied it, but I could never get you or any other minister to adequately explain the difference of the God of the Old Testament and the God of the New Testament. How can a rational person believe it is one God?

Edward: I laugh out loud every time I witness you explaining to a class that the only way you were able to accept that concept of one God in the Bible was if God was a woman who went through menopause and got over being pissed off and became all loving.

bj: It was the first thing I asked my soul once I made contact with Matthew, my first guide. I asked him to please explain the Gods of the Bible. He said the Bible is a book of history, of two different times in history. That at the time of the Old Testament the being holding the position of Lord of Earth was Jehovah and the time of the New Testament the Lord of Earth was Yahweh and that Jesus came to prove the ascension and to bring the energy of the Cosmic Christ Consciousness to Earth. Of course, I wanted to know why that wasn't the way it was taught in the churches. He explained that the people who edited and translated the Bible were church leaders who wanted to make sure the people remained afraid and controllable by those who were in religious control.

bj: At the time, I was somewhat relieved to realize I was not wrong in believing they were not one God, but pissed off that we had all been lied to about the real truth. Matthew also tried to explain the Spiritual Hierarchy to me and that really upset me at first to think the Universe is run by a corporation of higher level beings who had once been Human and had graduated and ascended like Jesus. I felt that and the Oversoul were certainly truths we should have been told. I felt like I had been lied to by so many religious teachers throughout my life that I never wanted to enter another church.

Edward: I know what you mean and, in my case, I felt worse because I had not been teaching the truth. I had also been lied to. I tried to sort out what Jesus had taught and to begin to rethink the whole thing, but it was confusing to say the least and is part of what led me to quit the priesthood.

Here, we are not only taught about the Spiritual Hierarchy, but are taught by the members of the Hierarchy who come here to instruct. You have gone a step further in your progression by directly communicating with them and writing down what they give you to teach and performing the missions they ask you to do.

Here, we are also taught science and where science and Spiritual Law meet. I am told that eventually this will also happen on Earth, but much of what is taught in the churches as religious truth is going to have to be exposed as methods of controlling people before people will begin to be exposed to the truth. More and more people are incarnating who are only willing to think for themselves, but there are still masses of Humans who do not trust thinking for themselves or don't want to go to the effort it takes to have an original thought.

We were taught that the devil and hell exist and that people are born into sin. Neither exists as we were taught. So much of what we were taught, even through Bible stories beginning when were children, is myth. It is interesting to observe now how the entertainment industry is beginning to project the idea of Masters of the Universe and beings from other civilizations. As I said before, I have not as yet visited other planets nor met with other civilizations, but I do look forward to being able to do so.

Angels are another level of life we become acquainted with here, but their vibrations are so high that they usually cloak themselves energetically when they come here to visit. The teaching of the Angelic Realm is left out of the religious teachings on Earth other than the mention of a few Angelic messengers, which is a shame. Knowing the different levels of Angelic life and about the Elementals and Devas should be taught on Earth as well as the information about colors and vibrations.

I am thrilled that you took on the project of describing the 49 Rays and their Meanings and Uses for the Spiritual Hierarchy. What a challenge, but you stuck with it until you brought it into usable form. This teaching is going to be one of the major spiritual breakthroughs of the Aquarian Age.

We are taught in the Universities here about the different levels of Angelic Life and about so many things that are not mentioned or even thought of as necessary information on Earth. Waves of energy are now being sent to Earth to deliberately cause Humans to begin to question what they have accepted as truth and what they've been taught. There is hope now that more truth will begin to be taught not just through religion, but throughout the educational systems on Earth.

I've been told that the entire Human state of consciousness will enlarge to be able to think of more than one thing at a time. Such a thing seems inconceivable to Human minds, but once the limited image on Earth is broken, the soul will learn to fuse not only with one's soul mate, but with the souls of one's particular group unit; much like what you are doing and teaching of the Oversoul and Oversoul communication. We are told that eventually we will be able not only to think our own thoughts, but also that we will be able to embrace the entire thought concept of our Oversoul. This is such an exciting idea.

bj: Can you explain prayer as it operates on your side?

Prayer can be one of the most vital activities ever undertaken, and because it sets so many forces into operation, it is well to understand the spiritual mechanics involved. Maybe you wonder to whom should you pray; to your guides, your soul or directly to God? Prayers should be directed through to God. Nothing can be brought about unless sanctioned by God, and nothing happens contrary to God's Laws. If you pray to spirits you would also be contacting God within them, so it does help to talk with your guides or your soul so they are aware of your needs and desires. It may be through them that God will manifest the answer to your prayers.

It is good to always call upon the spirit of God. It is good to pray for spiritual understanding and further unfolding of your spiritual gifts. It is important to pray for only what is desirable. Prayer for an object or a circumstance that would deprive someone else so that you may attain what you desire is objectionable. Such a prayer may attract spirits who will aid you in accomplishing your purpose, even though they may be aware that attaining your prayer will only decrease your happiness later. Praying to your soul eliminates this possibility. The soul always has your highest good in mind. It is important when you pray for a change of circumstances that you ask for the outcome to be to the highest good of all concerned.

Prayer is not just an expression of a desire, as you phrase it; it is putting a purchase order into the Universe almost like an advertisement. We on this side welcome the opportunity to help and when we serve you it also serves us in our progression; it serves a mutual purpose. You should put it in writing and be very exact and precise in the wording of your desires so that nothing can possibly be misunderstood. Again it is best to express your desires in prayer directly to God.

Prayer is an active form of creating. It is to be active both mentally and physically and the one praying is expected to do their share in holding the vibration and image clearly of the desire. They are also expected to do any act of faith the soul intuitively suggests to them.

Everything operates here according to Divine Law. Some prayers can be answered instantly, if the circumstances can be instantly harmonized. Others require a slower action of natural processes. Some prayers may not be answered at all or the response may be "no." When this happens it is because those wiser than you recognize the lack of wisdom in the request and, realizing what the results might be, withhold their help. I know you have asked Saint Germain for large sums of money with which to help others and he has attempted to explain that he believes that would change your life too much from your true mission. I know that you continue to disagree with his assessment and believe you could handle it appropriately.

Your prayers can only be answered to the measure of rewards you have earned though your own thoughts, service and actions. In a way it's like creating a bank account by doing good deeds and later asking to withdraw from your account. Granting or not can also be directly connected to the person's karma and the amount of light one carries in the vibration of their body.

When you give help, service or funds you are adding to your own account and then when you have a need or a desire the soul has an account to draw from to fulfill your desire. There is also the situation of karma. Sometimes when you pray there are people in your life who owe you karmically and it behooves them karmically to assist you. One cannot receive blessings without giving blessings.

There are those whose work on the astral is principally to deal with prayers expressed by those of you on Earth. They study the vibrations of prayers as Earth scientists study the vibrations of sound and light. Prayers are analyzed and separated and classified as rays of light. Memorized prayers are seldom spoken with enough emotion or energy that any response from a higher dimension actually happens.

The more mundane prayers are dealt with on the more mundane spheres, those closer to Earth, but those that contain light rays with which the lower souls are unable to deal, pass beyond their range, on up to the higher spheres to be dealt with by beings of greater knowledge and wisdom.

In some religions, the followers repeat daily that they were born in sin and their repeated words create a web of guilt around their bodies. These people often reply "I'm sorry" about almost everything that happens in their lives usually without even realizing they are saying it.

When a person on Earth prays for a person in the spirit world, that person feels the prayer and it helps them, especially if they are in the lower realms and working toward moving to a higher plane. Thoughts of pure unselfish prayer rise upward from the personality like a beam of bright light. Pure prayer force ascends slowly through the ethers, penetrating like electrical current to the one who receives the prayer and it blesses them.

I've witnessed you following your intuition, especially at the casino, to give funds to the person next to you because your soul suggests that person needs help. Sometimes you are the one chosen to answer that person's prayer. This also insures that when you are in need you are likely to be the recipient of help from higher forces or from the person next to you.

I've also witnessed your prayer for help with your physical body and its current condition. I'm sure it is difficult for you to understand why you don't seem to be receiving the healing you are requesting, especially since it limits your physical activities so much. I was grateful you were granted the contract extension and went through the open heart surgery, but it is puzzling why our Oversoul is not sending you more physical body help since you do so much for the soul and other people. I would recommend you continue to demand healing of the soul. I shall continue to send what I know to do to assist you.

    I have very much enjoyed our visits.

    Be well, my love, Your Edward

11.

Comments From Edward in the Afterlife

Edward was my fiancé who made his transition to the afterlife in 1979, four days after I moved from Texas to marry him. He was an Episcopal priest and my soul was concerned that if I was allowed to communicate with him in the afterlife I would still consider him my spiritual authority rather than attempting to communicate with my soul. Several years later the soul allowed me to communicate with him briefly. At that time we thought that we were to combine our efforts and to write about his experiences in the other dimensions. That did not happen. Now, he has been allowed to share with me what it is like where he is but only for this purpose.

Edward: Our love making that fourth night we were finally together gave me the energy to get out of my body. I do so regret having to leave you after such a short time of our finally getting to be together. I was so happy and more content than I had ever been in my life during that four days with you and your children. I'm glad I remembered to call you several times that day to tell you how happy I was, since that was our last day to be together on Earth.

I see you have recently written and taught about the Bardo in your classes. I did have to go through the Bardo because I had so much grief to work through about leaving you and the priesthood and so much anger still toward the members of the Vestry who fired me. I had so much grief and felt I had been betrayed by so many people there at the church who had pretended to be my friends. Many days at the church I felt you were the only one on my side. The Vestry used the excuse that they felt I was no longer preaching from the Episcopal doctrine to let me go. At least that was the excuse they used. I now realize the events were created by us and our souls to get us both out of Lubbock and on to bigger missions.

I'm sorry you felt so betrayed by me after I convinced you to leave the security of your home and family in Lubbock. It did and does seem like such a harsh way to accomplish the soul's goal of getting us free to be who we really are. I did feel relieved when I found Bill Browning after I was over here and got permission from the soul to encourage him to help you with starting the greeting card business. Your artistic ability has continued to grow through the years and I am grateful you still make your lovely cards and share them with others. The energy you put in your paintings and cards blesses those who receive them.

I am so proud of you and all you have accomplished for yourself and our collective Oversoul. Your efforts have caused all of us in the Oversoul to grow wiser and stronger and to move into higher dimensions. What one aspect of the Oversoul does, helps all the other members of the Oversoul.

I was helped by the counselors who work with those of us who are newcomers to this Otherworld to forgive those I felt had betrayed me and the grief I felt by having to abandon you after convincing you to give up your security in Texas.

It has been difficult because the Oversoul has not allowed us to be in communication. I felt so powerless to help you deal with so much grief you were experiencing being separated from your children, your friends, the church and everything you were used to in your life in Lubbock and your Mother's death at the same time. I was so angry and disappointed with the Bishops of Texas and Oklahoma and their treatment of you. Their attitude that you had killed me by making love with me and their judgment of our leaving our families to be together was painful to watch. Their telling you that you were no longer welcome to take communion was such a misuse of their power and an expression of their egos that I was even more disappointed in them and I had even more anger toward them.

I was stuck in the astral for awhile until I worked through the grief and anger. I've been allowed to attend many classes and to be present for many teachings from the masters through the years, which has fulfilled my thirst for the truth and gained more awareness that much of what we were taught in seminary and teach from the Bible was not the truth. Ignorance of teaching untruths is forgiven here once we are exposed to what is truth.

I remember you enjoyed cooking and always brought delicious meals to the potlucks we had at the church. Newcomers here often eat and drink as we did on Earth. They still feel the need of food and drink. It takes a while to be aware that all we have to do is breathe the etheric substance from the air as nourishment. Believing we need to eat and drink was a hard habit for me to break and to accept that all we had to do was breathe. That which we do consume is discarded as vapors rather than waste matter from the body. Nourishment and life force are absorbed as we absorbed air and sunshine or light on the Earth plane. Here, the air itself holds an essence containing all the qualities necessary for the nutrition of these new forms. Cosmic light emanating from higher planes pervades the lower planes and it is this cosmic substance that nourishes our spirit.

When we do choose to eat and drink, it is for fellowship and it is mostly the amazing fruits that grow here that we eat and the juice from the fruits that we drink. The fruits such as plums, cherries, grapes, grapefruit and melons grow without anyone needing to tend them. When they are picked, they are immediately replenished.

You will love the flowers here even more than the ones you grow and see on the Earth, my love. Their beauty and fragrance are amazing. Everything here is created mentally. When we have a need or we desire anything, we just hold a focus and intention on an image of the thing and that energy and focus cause the thing to appear. Creating things mentally or learning to manifest what we desire is something that we learn to do gradually. It is one of the first things we are taught in the Halls of Wisdom. It takes a while to become proficient at it. I've witnessed that this is one of the things you are teaching there to the people in your classes and I am grateful that you are helping them to be more advanced when they make their transitions to here.

bj: What kind of clothes do you wear and where do you get them?

Edward: Our clothes are also created by our thoughts. We can create clothes like what we wore on Earth in the beginning, but of course, since I hated wearing suits and ties that's not what I thought about. I was also through wearing black and a collar like when I was a priest so at first I created shorts and t-shirts since the climate here is warm and pleasant. I loved the freedom of not having to wear a "uniform." Now I have learned to create robes, not like the ones I wore as a priest, but these are more comfortable since we don't need to wear underwear. Sometimes I make them out of what we would think of on Earth as silk or even a lighter fabric that's available here but not on Earth.

Colors are way more varied here than what is available on Earth, since the light spectrum here creates colors not seen on Earth. Color and what the colors represent vibrationally are important and taught here. We are free to wear whatever we choose, but most folks choose full length flowing robes. The creative designs are limited only by the scope of our imagination.

Creating clothing or anything else requires a clear mental pattern and shape and a lot of mental focus to hold the vision of the desire to draw the energy and power to actually materialize it. In the higher dimensions, materials assume the appearance of silk, velvet, gold cloth, shining lace, or gauzy, gossamer veils, but I don't choose any of these adornments. The higher the plane the less the fabrics are like those on Earth; in the higher planes the fabrics become almost transparent with luminosity.

In the higher planes the clothing reflects the level and station of the spirit and some of the masters wear jewels and symbolic colors of their station. Changes of clothing can be automatic according to one's thoughts or emotions or can be a matter of the will of the person according to their preferences. Clothing more or less reflects our inner character. On Earth we wore clothing to protect our physical bodies from the climate we were in. Here clothing is worn more as a symbol of the spiritual condition or station of the wearer.

Each plane contains its own vibrations; therefore, the clothing substance of one plane might be completely different from that of a higher plane. The substance is gathered by the will of the personality from the atmosphere, from the flowers, from other forms and magnetically treated until it evolves into the shape, beauty and perfection held in the mind of the one creating. This is taught in the schools.

In the planes of the masters the clothing almost appears to be part of the being and they often wear crowns with jewels and jewel encrusted girdles around their waists and radiate energy from their crowns and ornaments.

In all things we are the creator of our own clothes, homes and surroundings here. We tend to gather and live near others who have similar interests and desires for learning. It is easy to recognize others who are similar in nature and thoughts by looking at their auras and the way they choose to dress. I tend to spend lots of time at the university and in the libraries when I'm not on duty in lower realms helping newcomers to adjust when they first leave their bodies and helping them locate their friends or members of their family who have come across before them. I've been allowed to travel to the astral to help, but only occasionally as I am still learning how to be of service without trying to influence or control others.

I've learned a great deal about controlling my thoughts and emotions since what we think here is obvious to others in a way that is much more apparent than it is on the physical plane, almost as if our thoughts and emotions are transparent to others. At first this is really unnerving to realize others are so aware of what one is thinking and feeling. But it is about our learning to control our minds and emotions. If we had been taught this while we were still on Earth there would have been less confusion in our communications, but our egos were so strong that we attempted to hide what we were truly thinking and feeling. Here we are more content and less judgmental.

The art of telepathy is not acquired without considerable effort. Once I reached Summerland, my communication with others became almost always telepathic. When I go into the astral to help others, I have to remember to actually speak aloud. Seldom, after being in spirit for a while, do we feel the need to speak aloud unless it is for the purpose of singing or chanting.

Once I reached Summerland, I learned to think and communicate in the universal language. In these higher planes even though different languages are spoken, the consciousness perceives and understands what the others are communicating. There are no language barriers. We have learned to be clairsentient and use the language of the heart. Here communication is more from soul to soul.

I've moved though several dimensions during my stay here and feel most at home in Summerland. The beauty here is remarkable and not easily described since it is so far beyond what we were used to on Earth. The weather is always perfect and there are no irritating insects. The plants all vibrate with energy and the colors are exquisite. Being in the flower gardens is such a treat since the fragrances and the energy of flowers is so uplifting and rejuvenating.

The longer I am here the more I understand that everything is a part of the Oneness, a gift and a part of the Source of all creation. I do wish we had been more able to understand this while we were on Earth. Earth and all nature there is so beautiful, but I think we became immune to its beauty because we were so focused on just living and making a living and getting along that we forgot to appreciate what was free and around us as the beauty of nature. I wasted a lot of time in worry and being concerned about what other people were thinking of me and not enough in gratitude for all we were freely given by God to enjoy.

I still seek to learn more everyday and to help others as much as I can. Here we never stop seeking to know more truth and to practice what we are taught. We can never reach a point where there is nothing more to learn. For most of us, our desire for knowledge never ceases.

Some days my routine is to guide newcomers to the area that matches their spiritual level of understanding. Our first homes here are prepared for us before our arrival. They can only be constructed according to our thoughts and actions while we were on Earth. My home now is open to the beauty of nature here in Summerland and is almost like living without walls. The home and the objects are all beautiful and inspire me to be increasingly more creative. I had barely begun to paint before I left Texas and now I go to art classes and find great joy in painting, especially with watercolor just as you do. Here we all attempt to create more and more beauty.

Homes in Borderland are not nearly as beautiful as those here in Summerland, since our homes reflect the level of our spiritual understanding, our thoughts and actions. Sometimes I am asked to go to Borderland and help people there realize that only beneficial action for others can bring them real comfort and higher attainments. They eventually become aware that they must seek to help those who are vibrationally even lower than themselves. By helping others, a new light and a new consciousness begins to awaken within them. It is rewarding to do this service since I remember what it was like for me when I was there.

When we were in Borderland, we had to unlearn much of what we believed to be truth when we were on Earth, especially spiritual truth. When I was in Borderland we attended classes where truths were clearly defined. People who remained bitter or who seemed content with their lot did not attend classes, so they remained in Borderland far longer. Fortunately for most, sooner or later an interest begins to stir within them and eventually they seek to move up to a higher vibration and more beauty. Some people require many incarnations before they make it out of Borderland.

Many Borderlanders still cling to the worn out theology taught on Earth. They hold fast to unprincipled and arbitrary rules they had been taught by the church leaders and remain stuck following those rules and thus remain in blind submission. They seem not to connect their theology of Earth with their present circumstances, and continue to be willing to bow down to the mediation of others, still allowing religious leaders who are still practicing and teaching old theology to stand between them and their God. I often feel regret for my part in being their intermediary when

I was in that position as a priest. Part of what got me fired from the church was teaching we can communicate with God without an intermediary and by not following the Book of Common Prayer.

Many people in Borderland still visit old confessionals, whispering to presiding priests, concerns about the lives they are now leading, complaining of their terrible oppressions and begging for prayers to help them out of their troubles. There are still some priests here who serve them and do so fully and sincerely believing they are following the course of truth since they also refuse to go to truth classes that would contradict what they were taught to believe on Earth. They still argue among themselves that their truth is the only truth.

Usually, when Borderlanders begin to realize that there are better realms of life, they send out a prayer for a loved one who has gone before them for help and seldom is such a call ignored. That is how many Borderlanders are brought to see the light from higher worlds by connecting with others who have gone before and have reached a higher understanding. They cannot go with the person who comes because the difference in vibration would be too painful. They have to start deliberately raising their own vibrations by serving those who are beneath them vibrationally, in order to move upward, but at least they then realize there are other planes that they can eventually attain.

Only by serving others are we able to eventually graduate into the higher realms. We of Summerland visit Borderland regularly to encourage and help Borderlanders in every way we are allowed, but the length of time we are there is not long because it feels so dense to us that we are grateful when we get to retreat back to Summerland.

In the higher Borderland, the atmosphere is more rarefied, the elements are more ethereal. In these higher Borderland levels, inhabitants constantly go to the lower regions to instruct others. They quickly learn that only through such services do they help themselves.

In the Midlands there are not only private homes but also many buildings I can only describe as apartments. Groups residing in the latter either prefer not to be isolated in private homes for personal reasons, or they reside together to carry out certain missions.

In the Midlands there are birds, flowers and many fruits. There are some beautiful homes and well organized grounds. There are lakes and mountains and schools of instruction, but not as many as in Highlands and Summerland.

On the planes of Highland there is considerably more light. The homes are far more beautiful and the gardens and flowers radiate an unearthly beauty. Lakes are much larger and there are pleasure boats. Inhabitants there congregate to study the arts and there are colleges for various instructions very much like in Summerland.

There is beautiful music in Highland and Summerland. A great many inhabitants enjoy making musical instruments and playing them. I still play the piano and have a piano in my home in Summerland. There are mountains and streams and beautiful scenery in Highland and in Summerland.

On the planes of Highland, homes are symmetrical and artfully arranged, containing paintings, drawings and fine furniture. They walk as a means of getting around but some have also learned aerial flight. I've taken instruction in aerial flight, but as yet I have not mastered it.

In Summerland there are even more magnificent scenes and cities, rivers, extensive groves of amazing trees and lakes as clear as crystal. There are scientific institutions and laboratories. New inventions are created here and then impressed upon the minds of Earth inventors and researchers, but I spend more of my time in the arts, music and learning.

In Summerland, there are individual homes but many are arranged in groups. There are vast educational assembly halls, elegant meditation temples, colleges for astronomers, writers of poetry, books, music, and all artistic endeavors. Fountains of living water are everywhere and the flowers, as I have said, are beyond description.

In higher Summerland, where I visit occasionally, the scenes are almost beyond Human understanding. The homes there are mansions with extensive grounds and gardens. Flowers are more variegated and richly perfumed. There are arbors and vines and still more delicious fruits. Mountains are in the distance and the water in the lakes is transparent.

There are indescribable universities in these Summerland zones. Teachers from the celestial spheres are often here offering instruction. There are colleges relating to the laws of mesmerism, electromagnetism. Intuitional and inspirational influences are sent from Summerland to Earth, psychic and spiritual instructions are offered as well as meditation.

People from Summerland constantly descend to the lower realms to carry their messages of truth. It is from Summerland that most spiritual guardians of people on Earth are found. I am occasionally allowed, or better to say invited, to be a guide to someone on Earth.

There are many children who have crossed over that live in these higher vibrational areas. The children have guardians that live with them.

They also have teachers at the educational centers where they learn about nature, scientific principles, spiritual truth and controlling their minds and thoughts for manifestation. They also have amazing, fascinating, color-enhanced playgrounds built in such magnificent forms to expose them to geometry and mathematical principles. As the children achieve more and more understanding of these principles, the colors of the equipment change to indicate their progress and they graduate to new, and more complex levels of educational playgrounds. Other outdoor areas are available for scientific experiments to demonstrate natural laws such as gravity, photosynthesis, propulsion and more.

In Summerland there is only beauty. There are no insects other than butterflies and dragonflies. There are no beasts, only the animal pets Humans loved on Earth who join their Human once they have crossed over.

The joy of living here is beyond description. Poets have attempted to describe it, artists have tried to catch visions on paper and canvas. The very atmosphere here is mellow and glowing; everything seems to be breathing with a living force, even the greenery. There is never an upset, never violence. All here is tranquil and peaceful. Even the clothing here appears to shine.

In Summerland, people are busy pursuing truth. We understand the law that regulates our society and we harmonize with it. We understand the purpose of the soul is perpetual spiritual growth.

Everything in Summerland moves in perfect harmony. Over here we not only reap the good of what we have sown, we also experience the happiness we wished for but which we never seemed to master while we were on Earth. Again, I tell you that the four days I was allowed to spend with you were the happiest of my life there.

Some of the fountains here flow with what we call living waters. These are highly energized waters channeled from the lakes and rivers of the higher planes. There are some on the lower planes also, but those are fountains whose waters have medicinal properties that rejuvenate and regenerate.

A rainbow arch of transcendent splendor is suspended over higher Summerland and its radiating colors seem to weave circle within circle, forming an aura over the entire area. The living waters of the beautiful fountains are often raised to great heights, refracting many changing colors, and spraying a shower of silver droplet in all directions. Flowing with and through the waters are strains of celestial music.

Near where I live there is a central building shaped like a gigantic pyramid. It is pure white. It is seven stories high. The main floor is almost a city within itself. This is the grand social room where people gather for companionship and pleasure much as do people on Earth gather at their country clubs. The ground floor may be opened to reveal one huge pavilion, or it can be portioned to provide smaller rooms for various activities like some of the large conference centers on Earth.

On some occasions when the entire room is opened, there is dancing much like a festive garden party on Earth. There is music for dancing, both inside and out in the open gardens among the beautiful flowers similar to what you saw at Versailles when you were in France. Two of the walls are not enclosed. They are composed of archways covered with colorful flowering vines and evergreens. The room is furnished with sofas, chairs and tables, beautifully formed and exquisitely carved, again very much like you saw in Versailles.

The second floor is devoted to musical and dramatic presentations. Here we gather for symphonies, concerts, operas, dramas, vocal and instrumental soloists, ballet and even motion pictures which are multi dimensional.

The third floor is an art gallery displaying a most incredible collection more amazing than what you saw at the Louvre. There are reproductions of great masterpieces created on Earth, but not the reproductions of the crucifixion and the bloody war murals you witnessed in the Louvre.

The fourth floor is a museum of sculpture. Here also we see statues of prominent people, mostly Humans who became important through earthly fame; many are of great philosophers, musicians, statesmen, artists and initiates. The great hall itself is a work of art, covered with gold leaf and flowers, crystals and precious gemstones. The entire hall is a museum of spiritual antiquities.

On the fifth floor is a library. There are other libraries about Summerland, but this is the most extensive. This one contains treasures seldom found on Earth. These are the manuscripts written by Masters and initiates. A few of these priceless manuscripts may still be found on Earth, but most are hidden. Most have long since been completely destroyed by Humans. Here, there are fresh, clean copies as if they were only recently written. This is one of my most favorite places to spend time studying the works of the Masters.

The sixth floor is devoted to special classrooms for teaching meditation, psychic development and spiritual illumination. Here teachers gather to instruct those who are interested in developing God-realization.

This is a very busy floor since many people of Summerland are interested in such an achievement.

The seventh floor, the capstone of the pyramid, is the most important of all the great rooms. This is the sacred hall of worship. Lectures are offered here conducted by the Masters from upper planes that are qualified to teach.

This is the smallest of the great halls. Seating is arranged as an amphitheater, succeeding rows above and behind each other. Many hundreds of people can be here at the same time. The seats in no way resemble uncomfortable stadium seats. They are more like cushioned lounge chairs, joined together, yet structured so that they collapse in order to be put away when more room is needed. Here we express our prayers, our aspirations and our profound gratitude to God, the Giver of All Life.

Etheria includes Borderland, Highland, Summerland and Paradise and it is just as natural a world as is the solid world where you live. It has its laws and we can view the stars. We have everything you have because everything on Earth that is not reabsorbed by the Earth ascends to become a physical part of Etheria.

This is such a wonderful world; there is little to behold but happiness. Even witnessing the trials and tribulations, like what you have been going through, does not necessarily bring us worry and unhappiness, because we can see the causes behind such actions and often can see the end of them. That is, we can see that the problem is going to end well, or we can see where the suffering involved was brought about by one's own thinking or carelessness. We are not allowed to interfere with Freewill, but can do our part to limit the suffering if our help is sought.

In observing a Human I know and care for who is experiencing sorrow, I feel sorrow to some degree, but not for myself. I feel it as compassion for someone else. I think it must be awareness that all things are happening as they should at all times; that makes a Human able to overcome their emotions and not be ruled by them.

bj: Why have you stayed out of a physical body for so long? It seems to me a long time to stay in the spiritual dimensions?

Edward: I have a mission here just like I did on Earth. Here I spend time welcoming and helping people who have just crossed over to adjust to their astral body and to help them find whatever help they need to begin to adjust. Many who cross over find it very difficult to believe they are dead. I work toward teaching them that they are not the body they left behind but that they are a unit of consciousness that never dies. I stay very busy every day, but I also let myself have time to just appreciate the beauty of where I am and I continue to be both teacher and student here.

I know you wanted to have me walk-in to another's body so we could be together again as a couple, but that was not and is not the will of the Oversoul. You work best alone, which is not a judgment but an observation on my part and the opinion of our Oversoul. You are so independent and determined to accomplish your mission, there is really no time for you to have a romantic relationship in your life at this time. You still have much to accomplish, so much to get out into the World from the wealth of information you have obtained from the Masters in the last thirty-eight years. I am relieved to see others reaching out to assist you to get the books you've written and especially the 49 Rays of God information out and available to more people in such a beautiful way as John and Belinda have accomplished.

Several others have helped financially and by editing what you have brought through from this side of the veil and of course Judi's and Ann's help in obtaining a home for you and a home for Namaste. I regret that I did not make sure you had a home before I left. Cindy and Farris created and offered a place to make your books available and a format for you to offer what you've learned to their group. This is indispensable to our Oversoul and your work with the Hierarchy.

As I said, I have not mastered aerial flight as yet, but we have other conveyances here; one is like a flying carpet. I have not as yet traveled to other planets in person, but I currently attend classes to improve my clairvoyant vision to begin to see the other planets and what takes place there. I know you are much more knowledgeable about other civilizations and planets than I am since you came back to Earth from another civilization beyond this solar system.

Hopefully, the Oversoul will allow us to continue our discussion in the future. I have so enjoyed getting to visit with you like this and to share some of what goes on here. I intend to remain in Summerland unless our Oversoul points out that I could be of more service elsewhere. Adonai, Dear One. Be well. Be happy. Your Edward.

12.

Comments from Edward in the Afterlife on Love and Marriage

Previous physical information about bj and Edward's meeting and life experience:

Edward: In our case our first physical meeting caused you to have a negative reaction to me as your new priest, not because of how I looked or my vibrations, but because of your previous experience with the priest who was leaving. He had never acknowledged you, or the work you did for the church, until the night of his going away party so you always had a negative attitude towards priests in general.

bj: That's true. I was so shocked that night of his going away dinner when I walked outside to get some fresh air, he followed me. He said, "I know I have never complimented or thanked you for all your dedication and service to Saint Christopher's. I've watched you and the way you care for your family and your friends and still do so much to help run the church. I apologize for not speaking to you before and not telling you how much I admire how you take such good care of your family and how much you do for others. I want you to know I am grateful to have known you and thank you for all your help."

    I was so shocked by what he said, since he had never before even acted like he knew I existed, that I was speechless. As if he was embarrassed by his admission he turned without another word and returned to the gathering happening inside the basement of the church. I think when I first met you I was concerned that you would treat me the same way. It took me several weeks and several encounters with you to realize how different you were from what I had previously experienced.

Through the years I learned to appreciate your attitude and attention, but I never took it personally or thought of our relationship as anything other than platonic and a working relationship. Since Martha and I had become close spending time together in the Women's Bible Study, I was aware of her unhappiness with you and your choice to be a priest; that puzzled me, but she and I never talked about it. When you announced that you were leaving Saint Christopher's and moving to Oklahoma, I felt devastated, abandoned and frightened that I would have to get used to yet another priest. Until then, I was not aware of my true feelings toward you or how much I depended on your always being willing to listen to me, really listen to me, and your encouragement.

The day you actually left for Oklahoma was the day my Mom had her second heart attack. I don't remember now if I called you or if someone else called you, but your calling me and offering to come back to help me to deal with her death astounded me. There was no way I was willing to inconvenience you and Martha by expecting you to return just for me. You had visited my Mom in the hospital at the first of the week when she had the first heart attack and she refused your offer to pray for her. At that point I think I realized she did not want to live. The day I came by her house and she was just returning from driving herself to the doctor I knew intuitively that she was going to die, but I denied it.

The letters you began to write me to help deal with her death were confusing to me, because no one I had ever met had ever paid so much attention or concern for me or my feelings. John had even expected me to entertain his sisters-in-law the night of Mom's funeral while he took his brothers to see some piece of machinery he had just purchased and my father expected me to give my Mother's clothing away the afternoon of the funeral to his sisters who had come for the funeral. Both of their attitudes were so unconcerned with how I was feeling that your concern for my personal feelings was foreign and confusing compared to how I had always been treated by the men in my life.

Of course, neither of us knew at the time that our souls were attempting to work out a bigger plan for both of us. The following eight months of your phone calls and almost daily letters were consoling, but when you first admitted how you really felt about me I was astonished and afraid. When you told me you were getting a divorce I was even more concerned. I did not want to be the cause of your marriage ending. The wording in your letters must have come partially from our Oversoul, because during those eight months I know I changed. I knew I was going to leave, but I felt so much guilt and confusion about how it could affect other people: John, the children, my friends at church and my reputation. I know I could have never left if my Mom had not died at that point.

Once I made the decision and John became aware that I was leaving him, he tried to change and pay attention, but by then it was too late. The comparison between how he had treated me and what you were offering me made it possible for me to go through with leaving. Your death seemed so cruel after so many months of my indecision about coming to be with you. The two Bishops calling to excommunicate me and to tell me I was not welcome to attend the funeral, because of my choice to be with you, added to the grief that was already overwhelming. The next day I was in a fog when John came and took the children back to Texas to live with him. I knew I was in no condition emotionally, physically or financially to take care of them without your help. His offer for me to return with him was kind, but I knew I could not face the consequences of my choice by returning there.

Those first few weeks of being alone with no one to talk with were so painful. I was so full of guilt, remorse, grief and pain that I feared for my sanity. The only thing that helped was sitting still and praying, but no response seemed to come from God. At first I felt I had made the worst decision of my life, but going back was not a choice for me.

Back to Edward's impressions of Summerland:

bj: I would like to know more about love in the Afterlife and the death of the physical love between married people, when they each seek physical fulfillment outside the marriage, as we did? And what about people who have known more than one deep, true love, but lost through death, which love will we be with? I want to rejoin you when I crossover, do you think that will be possible? I do think we will be allowed to be together again at some point.

Edward: It will all depend on the needs of our Oversoul. You've done so much work on yourself and learned so much about spiritual principles and raised your vibration much higher than most Humans so I'm sure you will enter Summerland quickly. I may even be allowed to greet you as you crossover.

Love here is so different than love on Earth. I will try to explain what I mean and this may sound like a lecture to you, but I will attempt not to be preachy. Actually every Human problem is directly or indirectly linked with love. All the problems of Earth are co-mingled with the love problem, not the sex problem, but the love problem. The majority of Humans think the most profound way to express love is by having sex. It will be important in this, the Age of Aquarius, for Humans to begin to equate Love with vibration rather than physical sexual acts. Sexuality on Earth has become degraded, partially by what is presented in movies and television.

Only as Humans learn the true meaning of love will the problems of Earth find solutions. Love takes a thousand forms. Love is Life, and life is Love. God is Love. With Etherians, love begins when two people become aware of the matching vibrations of the other. On Earth, Humans usually connect through sight, how they appear physically to each other is what attracts at first connection.

Humans will become more sensitive to vibrations as Human evolution advances. Then, when a person meets another, the wavelength of their vibrations will stir a response even before they have time to see the details of the other's physical body. When a wavelength harmonizes vibrationally with your own it cannot help but stir a response. Most people are not aware that the first question to ask their soul at that point is, what is the purpose of this relationship? The vast ethers of space contain millions of vibrations, flowing outward on specific wavelengths, seeking corresponding wave lengths.

Every Human form possesses its individual antenna which, like the rotating radar antenna at the space tracking station, is forever subconsciously 'feeling' for its mate, seeking to find the beloved. As powerful dynamos and electric batteries, charged by the constant flow of mind and soul energy, Humans perpetually project streams of thought and emotion. Frequently the current is short circuited, failing to find a proper connection to a matching frequency. Too often this projection of subliminal consciousness makes contact only on a physical level. Rarely, but sometimes the contact also synchronizes on the mental and spiritual levels as ours did, even though we attempted to ignore and avoid it.

Often the attraction, on the Earth plane, begins prior to an actual physical contact. It begins with an exchange of vibrations. It is difficult on Earth for a Human to recognize whether the exchange of vibrations goes beyond the physical. This is especially obvious with the new method of seeking a mate through the computer matching sites. The person can sometimes connect to the vibrations of the person's ad without ever having encountered them physically, but the vibration may not be as clear if the reader only considers the words of the sender and not the vibration. Words can be deceiving more than vibrations.

Over here 'antennae' are far more sensitive. The reading of another's aura is more simplified. Therefore, our approach to love is considerably beyond the contact of body with body; it is more energetic, more vibrational. When Humans have developed more intuitively, they will begin to feel beyond their physical responses. Humans will then begin to instinctively and intuitively recognize one whose aura harmonizes with their own on all levels.

In the future, Humanity's more sensitized spiritual antenna will make it possible for them to recognize the polaric vibrations that correspond and harmonize with their own. Seeking the corresponding polaric vibrations, they will recognize it by their psychic senses which will be stronger than a physical reaction to another. In all things, particularly in love experiences, Humans will begin to use their "psychic filters or discernment."

Marriage in Etheria is a much more cautious procedure than on Earth. The astral form, being a much more sensitive 'radio,' will not become promiscuously involved with another who does not harmonize vibrationally. Over here the searching for a mind-to-mind polarity is as important as a body-to-body polarity upon Earth. Unless there is this vibrational connection spiritually and mentally, the sharing of a personal love is out of the question.

I feel that shortly after you and I met we were a match emotionally, mentally and spiritually and only when we finally got together physically was it obvious that our vibrations were fully compatible even though we did not then understand the even deeper connection of being projected from the same Oversoul.

On Earth it is easy to be so attracted physically to another that one or both can totally ignore the fact that in many other areas they are not well matched. Often they marry quickly without considering many other parts that may not match up until they are living together and attempting to compromise to make the union last. This is what causes so many divorces, plus the fact that people are in a constant state of change, with some evolving and some not, so that to remain with one choice is often very difficult if not impossible.

One of the most important parts of Earth life is the frantic search of men and women to find the one special person to love. Historically on

Earth, there has existed an intangible relationship between love, sex and sin. The basic concepts of sin on Earth do indeed revolve around sex. The highest connotation of love between man and woman is the union of the two persons involved. This union is the highest physical expression of their mutual affection, but it is often entered into prematurely before they actually "know" each other well.

Historically, sex was not talked about openly now sex is a subject in almost daily conversation and public exposure of sexual relationships is currently exploited in the media. Many enter into sexual encounters with virtual strangers as casually as shaking hands. Sex was once a symbol of highest love, but now on Earth it has become cheapened for many. Sex and sin are no longer synonymous.

When a Human first arrives over here, they may find themselves in the lower astral planes where eating, sleeping and sex are continued much as they were on Earth. However, as they progress higher and enter Summerland, where things are much more mental than physical, they will find that sex and sexual organs are different since their new form is more refined than their Earth form.

Just as the newcomers realize that there is no need for nourishment from food in the same way they ate on Earth, they also discover that mating is expressed through more ethereal methods. On this plane we are capable of experiencing pain and pleasure, joy and despair, as we did on Earth, but such expressions transcend those of Earth.

On the astral there is no love-sex-sin trinity. Etherians accept beyond question that a man or woman can love more than once. On the lower planes there is no permanent marriage nor is anyone given in marriage. People here meet, fall in love, just as men and women do on Earth, and express love together. Frequently they marry, but they recognize that these marriage ties may not endure. They take each other for better or for worse so long as they both shall love.

On Earth, sometimes a couple stays together, sometimes they divorce and many times remarry several other times during one incarnation. The principle or difference between the astral practices and Earth relationships is that such unions upon Earth often bring forth children and here they do not.

On Earth, Humans degrade love to lust, whereas on the higher astral two persons cannot and do not mate who do not express the purer emotion of love. On Earth, having exhausted all the happiness each can give the other, they divorce, often with love having turned to bitterness or even hatred. On the astral, a couple meet and love, and stay together until they, too, have exhausted the love force. Unlike Earth, however, instead of this being a matter of a few months or years, it usually spans the Earth equivalent of scores of years. On the astral, when a couple has run the usefulness of their spiritual and emotional experiences together, they cease to be a couple. Each has contributed to the emotional and spiritual growth of the other, and each is released to find greater fulfillment.

When the love force specifically generated by two people here is spent, they part, remaining good friends, and each goes on to other loves. No soul is the property of another. Each soul is free. Each soul belongs only to themselves. Over here soul progress is the principal purpose of beings, just as it is meant to be on Earth.

Over here no one 'sticks together' to save a marriage, to save face, or because to separate would be a sin. Here it is considered a greater sin to stay together when love and respect is no longer present in the relationship. Staying together without love would only result is spiritual stagnation.

On Earth, these things cannot hold true because Humans on Earth face different sets of rules and responsibilities. When they bring forth children from the marriage union it is the children who should be given first consideration. The unions here do not create children.

On Earth, many karmic ties are created. In the Aquarian Age karma will not continue to be brought forth from one life to the next. This is the reason many people are having serial relationships to finish karma from past relationships. This is why new ways of thinking and attitudes are being developed concerning love, sin and sex.

Women seem to be gaining freedom from the fears which have bound them into marriage: the inability to financially provide for themselves, the ban lifted for women to be single parents by choice, and the need for male protection physically.

As the Human forms become increasingly refined, sex will gradually lose its connection with sin and become increasingly merged only with love. In the Aquarian Age, the creative powers will be lifted out of the reproductive organs up into the brain and Humanity will find itself expressing less animalistic sexuality and more of mental bliss.

As Humans individually experience genuine spiritual trips without the use of drugs they will come to realize how animalistic much of their physical expression of sex is and they will transmute more of their creative energies into mental enfoldment. Their drive for sexual expression will transmute to creative expression through the stimulation of the bliss center in the brain.

bj: This has certainly happened for me, which has been very interesting and freeing.

Edward: Yes, I have witnessed this in your growth. You no longer seem to be seeking a partner for companionship or for sex. This is also a result of your spiritual growth.

Many Humans as they evolve will begin to learn the proper role of sex in their spiritual growth. As more Humans turn to meditation and mysticism, as you have, their love of God will diminish their search for promiscuous sex and coupling will become increasingly unimportant as their creative forces will be more focused on creative expression.

I am aware that many people on Earth are still partner seeking and the possibility of marriage and wedded bliss. What is rejected here is the idea of two people remaining together after there is no longer love keeping them together. When the relationship becomes more of just a roommate situation with no true spiritual communion involved and more indifference is involved, it is important for the couple to separate. When compatibility is no longer possible, the couple should separate and make an effort to remain friends and be civil to each other.

Unlike Earth Humans, as Etherians we live by love and love alone. Any hatred over here is relegated to the hell planes. On the higher astral the Law of Love is the Law of Life, simply because those who have ceased to love part. They never allow the emotion of love to degenerate into mere tolerance or indifference. Etherians associate sex only with love, while too frequently Humans on Earth associate sex only with pleasurable release.

Humans of Earth have too long been scolded for finding any happiness in sex of itself. Humans, for the most part, are now emerging from the puritanical pretense that sex is only for the purpose of making children, not love. Sex is not sinful here. Since Love is the Law of life over here, sex love plays an important basic part of life. I personally am choosing celibacy at this time. Living in the vibration of Summerland invokes vibrations of an ongoing bliss that is even more satisfying than a sexual climax. I know you may be surprised to hear that I am celibate since you knew me to be very sexual. There is really no such thing as 'making love' since love cannot be made-it just is. Sensual sexuality cannot make love. As you and I both know from past experience, to simply experience the sex act is not necessarily to experience love. The sex we finally had together was definitely filled and fueled by love.

I often laugh when I hear you tell your class the joke about the Pope coming over here and talking with Saint Peter who assures him that because he has spent his life in spiritual service he is free to go and do whatever he chooses here in heaven. The Pope asked to be led to the library where he can read the original scrolls from which the *Bible* was translated. He enters the library and stays for several days and one day he runs out of the library waving his arms and declaring, "In the original scripture it is not celibacy that is demanded it is that we celebrate."

In looking at the rules as they apply to love over here and love on Earth, it is noticeable that a great deal of what is considered moral on Earth regarding sex is actually immoral on the astral and that which is immoral to Humans on Earth may be a way of life over here. To Etherians, sexual living together without love degenerates into the worst kind of sin; the worst kind of lust. Such a union is not a true marriage, on the astral, for marriage should be, above all, the union of love. When love has ended, Etherians consider it the highest type of wisdom to part as that no valuable cosmic time is given in useless frustration.

When love ends, evolutionary progress between a pair ends. One cannot contribute one iota to the soul evolution of the other. It is not so simple among Humans on Earth, because of the children that the couple has created.

It is because Earth does present challenges and obstacles that Humans continue to return to the World of matter. Humans will need to begin to try harder to attain spiritual knowledge and to live spiritually while still in their physical forms. Humans, as they evolve, will begin to remember the feelings generated between lives in the higher dimensions and begin to seek spiritually earlier in life.

It is true that Humans can accomplish more soul development in an hour on Earth in a physical form than in a year in heaven in a spirit form, because in the realms of heaven there are no challenges or conquests like what are found on Earth. There are not the same kinds of obstacles here against which mind and spirit can strive and grow. Life is much easier here. On Earth there is striving, growing, struggling and therefore the soul can make more progress on Earth in 70 or 80 years than it can here in hundreds of years.

Now that the sixth race is incarnating on Earth, through Human evolution these souls will have some memory of the freedom of the higher planes and in time will find some way to make the material aspects secondary and the love aspect primary. Their focus will be less on striving to succeed and to accumulate material assets. Over here we need no daily bread, no payment for rent, for homes, for automobiles, for clothing. We are free to make love an innate part of our being and to reach toward the Divine Heights.

In the Lowlands, inhabitants remain convinced of the need for nourishment, for sleep, for the practice of sex as they knew it on Earth. On the higher astral the need for food is transmuted. We learn to absorb revitalizing energies through the pores of our new body and our sleep, if we need it at all, becomes a twilight dream state which refreshes and renews.

Two lovers of the higher planes find themselves participants in a depth of feeling impossible to attain in a physical form. Over here feelings, sensations and thoughts are transmitted to the other instantly. Communication is by telepathy and emotions are equally exchangeable by clear sensing.

As the Aquarian Age unfolds and the Sixth Race incarnates, Humans will be living in the Fourth dimension and the veils between the various dimensions will begin to be less dense; awareness of other dimensions will become more obvious.

When Humans drop their dense bodies they will enter spheres that are fueled by different laws of space and time. As they adjust to a World of higher dimensions, their love concepts will change along with other habit patterns that were there in the Three-dimensional World.

Each Age carries the Human life wave to a higher illumination and the individual Human continually requires new teaching and a larger intuitional insight into the Laws that govern here in the different dimensions. To truly understand life and love after death, it is useful to study them while you are still in the physical as you are learning and teaching others. The veils between our two Worlds are growing thinner, which makes our communication possible.

Remember when we once discussed the phrase, "Your young men will see visions and your old men will dream dreams?" This is happening and will continue to increase in this Age. Church dogma, which promises no immortality and no ascension, is fortunately doomed. The new religion will of necessity be a religion of love. Humanity must pass from adolescence to adulthood and be able to face the truth of their immortality.

There needs to be more education about true love in schools as well as in religion. Humans must learn that the creative instinct is an essential part of the Human nature, and they need to learn to express it wisely through creativity as well as sexual expression. Every Human, regardless of their sex life, would be wise to develop a creative outlet. The rise in creative energy sent to Earth is increasing during this Age and Humans will need to express it creatively. If the creative energy backs up in the Human body without expression, it invariably creates depression. The positive use of the Human imagination into creativity reduces the possibility of depression.

The teaching of Love as a science is necessary because Love produces mysterious chemicals and is a Human's most powerful instinct. Included with teaching the science of Love, there will need to be teaching of the meaning of music, of vibration, and of sound as they relate to Love.

As things are now, many of the younger generation have discarded age-old moral standards and have not as yet formed replacement with a new practical set of principles. They stumble blindly on the animalistic expression of lust; the dangers being that such an expression attracts the lowest forces of astral beings that are completely carnal minded and are incapable of expressing soul force or true spirituality. Only the well-springs of pure Love can bring the spiritual, mental and physical delights to their ultimate fulfillment.

On the lower astral, confusing situations are sometimes created when a Human arrives who has been married to more than one mate, having loved each. Occasionally there is dissension over just who is the wife or who is the husband. Although such matters are not taken to court, as they often are on Earth, there are experts to consult about such things.

First, the counselor encourages each individual to realize that they do not belong to anyone other than themselves. Usually, each is advised to live alone for the time being. This way each has an opportunity to discover for themselves the one they truly desire to share full time companionship with, or if they would prefer at this point to be alone. No one is obligated to pick up a husband or wife relationship just because it existed on Earth, where there is no true love.

The problem of having had two or more husbands or wives is usually solved by the pull of the stronger, finer affection. Each soul is eventually drawn to the one who is most compatible for the time being. Each love relationship we have encountered on Earth has helped us with our soul development. No experience is ever wasted.

It is possible to be deeply in love several times during the course of a lifetime, with each love bringing a new understanding to the heart. One may have been purely physical love, offering no emotional understanding. Another may have been a true love on a physical and emotional plane but lacking mental harmony. I am aware that you have experienced both.

The Human who goes from one love to another, one divorce to another marriage, is seeking always that love which will complete them physically, emotionally, and spiritually. Until such a love is found, one soul will outgrow the other, and the union often degenerates into disillusionment and disappointment, but knowledge and inspiration have been drawn from each experience.

The marriages that seem to last the longest are between people who have developed deep friendship with their mate and have chosen a partner who is equal spiritually. In marriages where one mate has outgrown the other, the one left behind will wonder why all efforts to bring happiness are futile. The only thing that can save the marriage is for such a partner to make increased efforts to seek spiritual growth striving to become spiritually equal.

Mating inequality cannot happen in Etheria because Etherians understand vibrational equality and they do not enter marriage as lightly as people of Earth. Here the spiritual stature of every soul is easily discernable, and only those two who harmonize on every level would ever consider marriage; therefore, partings here are rare. Unions here are usually long lasting.

Among Etherians no material factors enter, because on the astral there are no economic problems such as the ones that cause so much conflict on Earth. There is no battle for food on the table or clothes on the back, only for higher mental and spiritual progress. Life here is so much easier than the lives we spend on Earth.

I have so enjoyed being allowed to communicate with you now. Hopefully our Oversoul will see fit to have us be in communication again in the future.

Sleep well my love,
Your Edward

13.
Comments From Edward on Spiritual Gifts

Edward: I know you have been criticized and sometimes applauded for being 'psychic.' So many people do not understand that everyone is psychic. The ability is a latent talent in every Human. Nearly everyone has had psychic experiences, but not everyone is aware of them. Comparatively few use the ability consciously in their lives. Humans have the potential to gain the spiritual gifts of: discernment, prophecy, healing, clairaudience, clairvoyance, clairsentience, speaking in tongues and channeling. So many people are frightened by the very idea that they could know things without reading it or hearing it; by just 'knowing.'

I started receiving messages when I started meditating in 1979, but they were short, not like what you are able to receive. The pressure that our Oversoul applied to get me to continue to suggest that you move to be with me in Oklahoma did not come in specific messages exactly; just more like an insistent and repetitive feeling of urgency. I know it was a very difficult decision for you to make and when your communication began, you still had the biblical residue in your mind from your *Bible* study that everything psychic was evil.

Christians especially who take the Bible literally after reading Deuteronomy 18.9-22, forbidding consultation with "familiar spirits is an abomination unto the Lord" think everything psychic is evil. It should be remembered that this command was given by the priest, not by God. God gave a different admonition: *"If there is a prophet among you, I, the Lord will make myself known unto him in a vision and will speak unto him in a dream."* Numbers 12:6.

In Samuel 10:6 a prophet is described as a man upon whom the descent of Spirit of the Lord changes him from a 'normal man' into 'another man,' compelling him to speak words not his own, but those which 'the spirit shall give him, utterance,' Again this comes from the priests not God. History is full of attempts by the priests to restrain truth. Communication between Humans and Etherians is a huge threat to the priesthood.

bj: What they did to Joan of Arc caused me a lot of fear when this first began to happen with me. I think discernment has been my most valuable spiritual gift. I avoided speaking in tongues for years until I was offered the opportunity to do the energetic activations for people which involved allowing the spirits to speak prior to Earth language blessings for the client.

Edward: I know, my love, but you persevered and continued to do what you believed and were continually given additional spiritual gifts. You are braver than most when it comes to spirit communication. I know the book that was tossed of the shelf at you entitled *Psychic Energy* freaked you out, but you were brave enough to purchase it even though you were afraid. I laughed when you made the bargain with God that His answer would have to be on one page and it was.

I know you had a lot of questions about the *Bible* that I was not equipped to answer for you even before you made your connection with your soul. You questioned the idea that you did not see how the God of the Old Testament and the God of the New Testament could be the same God and I was unable to give you an adequate response.

I've learned Jesus the Christ is not God. He never professed to be. But He represents all the power of God necessary to change life on Earth. He has the authority to speak for God as do you since you understand the indwelling Christ within.

There are scientific conditions under which electrical communication from this World to yours happens. There are communications stations, if you will, where we can make contact from here to Earth. It does not happen automatically. Recent conditions have made it possible for the Masters to insert images and information into television, radios and computers on Earth. This will eventually be more and more prevalent.

Many newcomers here try to communicate with people on Earth before they have the energetic strength to make the connection. It actually happens electrically through the Human body's magnetic grid in the brain. Many spirits wish to communicate with Humans and want the drama of being a channeled spirit, but few admit they do not know the answers to the questions that Humans ask, so many just make up answers they think may be believed. This is why having the spiritual gift of discernment is so vitally important, especially while an individual is still on Earth. Death does not bestow some kind of omniscience to a spirit. It is important to challenge any information that claims to be channeled. I've heard you tell people this in your classes, which is good.

I am relieved you did not decide to become a medium but chose to work with our Oversoul and the Spiritual Hierarchy. Some persons who possess and express extrasensory faculties may operate as 'mediums' conveying energy and or information from other dimensions electrically. Séances and the use of a Ouija board most often attract astral level spirits who wish to speak; it is not information that should be trusted just because a spirit has enough energy to move a planchette or rock a table. I know you had firsthand experience of this when you and your friend tried the Ouija board and got connected to an astral spirit attempting to pass itself off as Babaji, an Indian saint, and once you made that connection, it was strong enough to keep you from being able to connect with your soul. What a scary way to learn the importance of the gift of discernment.

I am aware that when you started painting larger paintings the spirit of Georgia O'Keeffe offered to help you with your art work, and when you started writing the psychic mystery novel you attracted the assistance of Agatha Christie. Most artists, writers, inventors, public speakers and musicians attract higher level spirits who have interests in helping creative people. Beethoven, Mozart, James Taylor and many others admitted that they wrote down what they heard from spiritual sources. Inventors like Edison, Marconi, Bell and many others were inspired to bring timely inventions through for Humans.

I am glad that you have learned that you do not need to practice Clairvoyance, or to visualize in order to receive accurate information or to manifest. It is true that to see or hear spiritually is of a lower vibration than knowingness. It is best for anyone seeking spiritual communication to ask their soul for the vibration of knowingness.

It is best, in the beginning, for a person to accept spiritual or psychic gifts for their own use and not for public exposure of their gifts. When communication with beings on this side begins to happen, the Human's body may shake, they may have an intense emotional reaction, feel hot or cold, their hands may lift by themselves without the mind controlling them. These reactions usually lessen after a few sessions of communication with spiritual entities. It is important to only seek this type of communication only with levels of one's own Oversoul rather than random spirits or relatives who have crossed over.

If a person wishes to communicate with a deceased relative, it is still safer and more spiritually accurate to do the communication by connecting to their own Oversoul and requesting their soul to contact the relative. In most cases the relative, especially if they are a new arrival here, will not have the energetic strength or knowledge of how to make this type of contact. The most accurate spiritual information can always be gained by communicating with or through one's own Oversoul. It is a good policy for a Human to develop a telepathic rapport with a certain being within their Oversoul and make an agreement with that level of the Oversoul to be their communicator, gatekeeper or receptionist. This installs a fail safe level that restricts astral entities from approaching the Human attempting to deceive the Human that they are a high level spirit.

bj: That has been my experience with Matthew. He and I have moved gradually from 5th Dimensional to 8th Dimensional energetically. He and I have been in communication since the first day of my attempting to have spiritual communication. I've learned so much from him and through him that I could not have accomplished without his connections.

Edward: Yes and his soul aspect has continually raised its vibration and usefulness through that contact and as a result of all the spiritual work you have accomplished with your connections to the Spiritual Hierarchy and the Intergalactic Federation. What one level of the Oversoul accomplishes feeds energy, wisdom and advancement into all levels of the Oversoul. We have all gained and evolved as a result of what you have accomplished during your years on Earth.

Few people today are expected to be prophets since so many people are now available to channel. You realize most of what is appearing on the Internet as prophecy today isn't happening. There have been people for centuries predicting the end of the World and today it is even more cluttered with people predicting global electrical shutdowns and monetary changes breeding fear instead of wisdom.

The veils between dimensions are thinning and more and more people are and will begin to see visions and receive messages in dreams and sudden flashes of inspiration even when they are not seeking spiritual communication. Often it begins by them noticing repetitive numbers on clocks, watches and their cell phones. You have witnessed that a person can become psychic without being the least bit spiritual, but use their gift strictly for material gain. This is where a lot of this misinformation is coming from, people who enjoy the attention and love creating drama and fear.

Only in more recent years have spirits become aware that communication between these higher dimensions and Earth Humans is possible and the electrical methods used are still being perfected. The masters hold a high enough vibration that they can easily communicate, but those of us in a slower vibration have to go to a communication terminal to accomplish this. I know you are more used to communicating directly with the masters and so connecting to my vibration is slower than what you are used to.

Most people who cross over have enough energy to move something in a loved one's house to show they still exist or repetitively they can leave some kind of symbol like pennies or toothpicks or match sticks, something light to get the attention of a loved one. I know you often think of me when you see a cardinal. I understand there are inventors on Earth now who are attempting to create a device to make multidimensional communication possible. Traditionally a person has to raise the vibration of their brain frequency to make the communication possible between the soul and the body or between the Human body and a spirit.

It is a good idea for a Human to practice these spiritual gifts while they are still in body to improve their contact with their soul as well as to prepare themselves for an easier time once they have arrived here. Since there is no time here, the idea of setting a time for spiritual communication is a bit more complex than a Human might imagine. The soul is always available for communication, but not necessarily so with other spirits with whom one might wish to communicate.

Out of body travel or long distance viewing can also be useful for a Human to develop as it will enhance their abilities to adjust once there are over here. One can begin by focusing mentally on a place they know, holding the intention that a person will see or know what is happening in that place currently. After a few practice sessions one can tune themselves with a place they have never been but would like to observe. They may feel they are making it up in the beginning. One should not use this tool to spy on others. Everything spiritual happens as a result of intention.

Developing telepathic communication as a way of communicating with the Oversoul as well as with other Humans can increase one's ability to communicate with the spirit world. First, it is important to believe you can do it; then to try it on a regular basis. Again it happens from intention. Sometimes you may find it useful, if you want to connect with person at a distance, to say aloud 'attend, attend, attend' and then state the person's name out loud as you make the energetic contact.

Healing can best be accomplished by connecting mind-to-mind with the person one is attempting to help. Your book on mind-to mind-healing will be a huge help for anyone attempting to develop the gift of healing, especially if the healing is to be offered from a distance. With intention, the healer should mentally intend to connect their own mind, with the Universal Mind and then with the mind and soul of the person requesting healing. This gives the healer an advantage so they can get specific information telepathically from the soul of the one needing help. When helping someone who is present, the same method may be used which will give the one channeling the healing energy insight as to whether the problem is inherited or is there an emotional cause that may be corrected. Healing energy is accepted by the healer and mentally sent through the etheric thread to the one needing help. It is accepted by the one needing assistance only to the degree they are willing to accept help.

Operating empathically to obtain information from another person becomes very destructive to the emotional body of the Human. Soul-to-soul communication to receive information or insight from another person is much better and less destructive to the Human body. Merging with another Human's body to obtain information out of curiosity is against spiritual Law and creates negative karma. The grounding exercise you were given to overcome your own overly empathic emotional body when you first opened up psychically is extremely useful for beginners or anyone who is habitually empathic as are many Humans, especially women it seems.

Psychic enfoldment should never be undertaken as a game or hobby, but only seriously as a means of soul development. Much harm can come from "playing" in astral realms both for the seeker and for those with whom they might share their gained information.

I admire your dedication, your strength, and your clarity as you continue to trust and to bring through spiritual knowledge to share with Humanity. You are a blessing to me and to many.

Be well, my love,
Your Edward

14.
Consciously Facing Life, Death and Dying

Earth-life is a school and part of a far-reaching existence. Death is not the end. Most Humans fear death, whether they believe in an Afterlife or not; they fear the unknown. No one knows for sure what happens at the time of death. Christians seem to believe in a heaven or hell that is a place, and that good people go to heaven and bad people go to hell. Most people, no matter how good they've been, wonder about the judgment, the accounting that will be required of them about their life. Christians seem to believe that they will be judged and from that judgment a decision will be made to send them on to heaven or hell. In my understanding, from Spirit, we are never judged by anyone other than ourselves. At the time of our physical body death, we do review the life in relation to what we intended to accomplish before we came into this particular incarnation. I think it is important to realize that we will be the only one to judge our performance. I think that it is also an important part of reaching spiritual maturity to be your own authority, to be your own judge.

Recent scientific and psychological studies are attempting to unravel or reveal what actually happens at the time of death. In his book *Life After Death* by Dr. Raymond Moody he interviewed many people who had near-death experiences. Their stories were all similar. They moved through a tunnel, they encountered people who they knew were dead and they encountered a bright light. The interesting thing about people who have had near-death experiences is that they didn't stay dead for very long so their experience mostly relates the experience of the transition from living to being in another place, being out-of-body. Because these reports are only about the first stage of the transition, many people feel that life after death has not been sufficiently proven and still prefer to look at death as the great unknown. Many people who have experienced near-death experiences often return realizing they have wasted much of their life and are determined to live differently.

There is now enough interest in the subject of death that a separate science has been established called "thanatology. Its name is derived from the Greek word "thanatos," meaning death.

The one thing I've observed in conversing with what we would think of as dead people is that they quickly become conscious; well, maybe not right away, but certainly before long they can quit blaming God for the quality of their lives, that at all times they were the one responsible for the quality, experiences and circumstances of their lives. We understand at that point that each experience, whether painful or pleasant, was meant to serve a deeper purpose than what we realized or recognized. We quickly find that what we have been led to believe is not necessarily true.

We suddenly realize that "My body may be dead, but I am still very much alive." While we are incarnate, we would do well to acquaint ourselves with and understand the connection between our visible self and our invisible or intangible self. The sooner we understand that the invisible, intangible self is our real self, the sooner we can learn to appreciate that we are not our bodies; that our bodies are containers that we have been graciously given through which we and our souls can experience life on Earth. Once we grasp this as reality, we can begin to live consciously from birth to death and beyond.

It is important for us to learn the Laws of Creation, or what some refer to as the Universal Laws, in order to live our lives within the Law. Everything is based on these uniform Laws. The same forces with similar characteristics are at work within each atom of our bodies as is between the galaxies and solar systems. Once we learn these Laws, we begin to understand that we are "masters of our own fate." Death is a completely natural process, which proceeds according to firmly established intelligible Laws.

One of the main problems Humans have is that they are in the habit of regarding what is invisible as incomprehensible or even unnatural. We are constantly surrounded, actually permeated, by waves of the most diverse kinds without noticing them. It would, therefore, be absurd for us to deny that there are also realities beyond our senses. The very fact that we have such a concept as "the beyond" at all surely means that we are quite aware of the existence of such Worlds.

Darwinists, behaviorists and evolutionists are only concerned with the development of our body, its organs and our brains. But the real person is not their body. To assume so would be like failing to differentiate between the driver of a vehicle and the vehicle itself. There is something within us that is capable of being conscious of itself, which can think about itself and already distinguishes us from animals. This something can intuitively perceive not only joy and sorrow, love and hate, but also abstractions such as art and beauty. The part of us that intuitively perceives is the part of us that is actually Human and spirit. Its voice, its language, through which it makes itself known, is the intuitive perception. It is that welling-up that does not depend on external sensory stimuli, but flows forth spontaneously from the innermost depth of our being. Our spiritual knowingness has nothing to do with Earthly intellect; it comes from deep inner feeling. It is not the same as being highly intellectual. In fact, the intellect can retard our ability to receive spiritual guidance. Our intellect can attempt to talk us out of what Spirit is suggesting. Our intellect is only an instrument bound to the body, an instrument meant to enable the Sprit to manifest itself according to its nature in this Earthly World. The only living thing within the Earth body that keeps it alive is the energy given from the Spirit and the soul. The "soul" is not something independent that exists side by side with the Spirit; it is the Spirit clothed in ethereal substance.

There is another form between the ethereal soul and the gross material Earthly body; another form that is called the astral body. It is very similar to the Earthly body in its consistency; the astral body is the direct prototype of the physical body. Our physical bodies consist of neutrons, protons and electrons, as does everything else in and on the Earth. Radiation connects the elementary particles. When scientists attempt to seek smaller and smaller particles, they eventually find Light and Light moves in particles and waves. Our entire Earthly World and our bodies are formed, so to speak, from above downward. Everything here is a product of the process of condensation, the slowing of the vibrations of Light.

A few decades ago, the recognition of the theory of relativity, quantum physics, molecular biology or radio astronomy would have been ridiculed as fantasy, occultism or superstition. Yet, it is now proven that everything that appears to us to have the semblance of firmly-knit matter is scientifically proven to consist of radiation, of that incomprehensible something (Light) out of which the Universe at one time developed.

Going back to us, we have the gross material Earthly body – after that the astral body, which consistency comes close to the material body –

and finally the spirit/soul in its ethereal body covering. Now the soul is connected with the astral body, and thereby also with the physical body, through the "silver cord," which can be seen by some clairvoyant persons. It is a kind of ethereal umbilical cord. It is the channel for the influence of the spirit/soul on the physical body. These bodies are not blended, but rather united or fused into one another like a collapsible telescope and held together by radiation.

Nourishment holds the body and soul together. If the body becomes ill, then it is weakened. This means that its radiating-power, its radiation, also becomes weaker. The soul must sever itself from a body which has been forcibly destroyed, or from one ruined by disease or weakened by old age, when a body can no longer produce the strength of radiation that brings about such a magnetic attraction power as is necessary to contribute its share in the firm union between the soul and the body. These results in the separation of the material body from the astral body and the soul/spirit body; what we call death.

The soul and the body must both produce sufficient radiation energy to keep the two connected. It can also happen that the connection is severed because the radiation of the soul is no longer directed to the Earthly body with the necessary strength. If the soul determines that the ego in the body is not willing to allow the soul to use the body, the soul can withdraw its energetic support of the life.

When the body is asleep, it produces a different radiation that does not bind the astral body to the physical form, and a person can dream or move out of body to journey into other realms. This is only a loosening, not a detachment from the soul.

We know that micro-electric processes are constantly going on in our brain, the effects of which can be measured as brain current with the electroencephalograph. The brain currently cycles up to thirty times per second in the waking state, which is referred to as beta. In meditation, the brain wave frequency drops to about 10-12 cycles per second, which is called alpha. In sleep, the cycle can drop as low as a half a cycle per second. The heartbeat, respiration, blood pressure and body temperature also diminish. The body economy is maintained only on a "pilot light." This diminished body radiation makes possible the loosening of the soul. While the body is thus relaxed, we dream. We dream in delta.

We are all familiar with the stage between dreaming and waking, when conscious thinking is already beginning to set in, but when we are still unable to move the body. This stage is usually referred to as theta. We are just bringing the "soul" near and as long as the radiation of the body is still not strong enough, the soul simply does not have it fully "in its grip." It is like engaging the clutch in a motor vehicle.

All radiation manifests as vibration, is vibration. At the time of death, unless the body is destroyed by violence or mutilation, the exit process is accomplished smoothly and is a gliding out of the soul by slowly and steadily reducing the current of electromagnetic energy and finally switching it off and disconnecting from the body. The soul withdraws the astral body from the physical body at the time of death.

After the Earthly departure of the soul, the astral body always remains near the physical body, usually to witness the funeral or memorial service and the behavior of those left behind. The further the soul moves away, the weaker the astral body also becomes; and the ever-advancing severance of the soul finally brings about the decay and disintegration of the astral body, which, in turn, immediately causes the beginning of the decay of the physical body.

If a person is strongly focused on the Earthly, if they did not wish to know anything about continuing life after death, of an ethereal World in the beyond, then through their own attitude, the connection cord is very firmly knit and will be difficult to sever. The severance may then take many days, during which time such a person, because of the density of the connection cord, must still feel what happens to their physical body, so that, for example, he does not necessarily remain insensitive to cremation or burial. Many religions and races require a waiting period before anything can be done to the dead body.

If a person is striving for the Light and believes in an Afterlife, they can very soon become loosened from their body and are spared the pain of physical death. It is my experience that a person can create their own version of the Afterlife. When we leave, we go into a dimension filled with persons, beings, who vibrate at the same frequency that we do. This is what determines whether we experience what we would think of as heaven or hell. If the vibration is low, a person moves to a low vibrational dimension and is usually surrounded by persons who died in a state of anger or addiction.

It is important for us to completely release a person at the time of their death rather than to try to hold them close to us. Our emotional attachment can keep them from being able to ascend to their correct dimension. Sometimes the person feels so connected to someone in this dimension that they refuse to go on into their correct dimension until the person they feel strongly connected to is also ready to leave their Earthly body.

Death is actually a rebirth into a World beyond, from which we came. These dimensions are non-physical but still filled with life. To understand dimensions, it is sometimes helpful to think of radio receivers. Radio waves are comprised of wave-bands; medium waves, short waves, ultra-short waves. We bear within ourselves different "receiving and transmitting equipment" for different wave-bands in the form of the physical body, the astral body and the soul body. For this reason the "out of the body state" involves first a "switch over" to the immediately adjoining wave-band of a higher frequency.

The division between dimensions is not as sharp as in a radio-receiver; the transitions are smooth. Since the astral sphere is still very near the Earthly, the departing one, who gradually begins to change over to the "frequency band" of the other World, is at first still able to include both sides in their perceptions. Thus they can recognize the thoughts whose vibrations lie within this range, but they can seldom make themselves heard. They can still see and hear the Earthly. However, they can no longer make themselves perceptible. They feel themselves as still alive, but expelled from the living and may feel tremendous fear and loneliness. Those who are alive would do well to know that their thoughts and actions are still seen and heard by the deceased. Most, once they recognize they are dead, wonder why they pushed away thoughts of death as if it were not inevitable. We all have to cross this threshold one day. It is better to do it knowingly, instead of being pushed into the unknown. Where we go depends on the density of our etheric bodies, our spirit bodies.

When a person moves from one dimension to another it is like breaking the sound barrier; everything seems to speed up. The faster movement of vibration also increases one's ability to comprehend. In the World beyond, a completely different kind of knowledge counts; a deeper knowledge, soul knowledge. To acquire this kind of knowledge directly from our souls will serve us well when we move into other dimensions. Intuitive perception can only manifest in the Earthly body by way of the ethereal body.

What we acquire by learning is of use to the intellect; stored in the cells of our brain it remains behind with our physical body. Only what we experience, perceive intuitively, what moves our Spirit, enters into us; that alone can we take with us. Today, the whole of Humankind suffers from one-sided intellectual development. We accomplish splendid works of technology, but we lack the ability to control them, to use them wisely, because instead of letting ourselves be guided by the Spirit, we have left the guidance to the Spirit's Earthly instrument, the intellect. Thus we interfere everywhere in natural happenings without being able to foresee the consequences, because we lack the true knowledge of this Creation.

What happens when a new soul is coming in? The first movements of the embryo in the Mother's womb announce the connection to the soul that intends to use the body. It is my understanding that the soul only connects to the embryo by the umbilical cord, but does not fully inhabit the body at that time. It further connects at the time of birth and at about the age of 5-6-7, the soul fully connects to the body, usually around the beginnings of schooling.

Reincarnation as a normal belief was expunged from Christian creeds at the Council of Constantinople in the year 553, for purely political reasons, in accordance with the wishes of Emperor Justinian I. It is very difficult to control or threaten a civilization that believes in reincarnation. Certain men historically have decided what people should be allowed to believe. The Catholic Church and many of the Christian Churches are still telling people what they can and cannot believe. Ex-communication is still practiced today, but at least they aren't burning us at the stake.

Suicide is not an acceptable method of leaving the Earth before a person's contract has been completed. When a person commits suicide to get out of the problems and the life they have created, through their own choices and decisions, they must return to the Earth almost immediately and will not only be expected to finish the contract of the previous life, but will choose a much more difficult situation than the one they left through suicide.

Understanding death not only takes away our fear of death, but it can also take away our fear of life, living to our full potential. What is our purpose? Everything in the Universe has a purpose and we are no different. Our purpose is to create, co-create with our souls and to be conscious at all times of our souls and the desires of our souls to use these bodies that they created to serve the greater plan for Earth and Humanity.

Within each Human is a seed of divinity. We are not fully developed spiritually. This Spirit core within us is a seed-grain, a spiritual germ. Like every seed-grain it contains the full potentialities of its species, but it must ripen gradually. Our seed is rooted into the Earth. We are in the World of matter for the maturing of our species, the spirit. We are here to learn to recognize the power of the Spirit within us, and to strengthen it for conscious activity. The diversity we experience here on Earth is not possible in other spheres. It is this diversity of experience that facilitates our ability to spiritually mature. This is what makes Earth life so important. We are called to be the connecting link between the material World and the spiritual realm. We are called to be conduits through which the beauty and harmony of the higher World flows down into the Earth.

15.

The Bardo and the Levels of Life Between Lives

The saddest aspect of death is that so many people know so little about it. Most only fear and dread it. It isn't difficult to understand why people are reluctant to face death kindly. When we explore all the research into all World religions it reveals that the universal teaching was death, purgatory, the judgment, the end of the World and eternal punishment in hell. Although there has always existed a teaching of individual judgment immediately following death, emphasis both in dogma and in religious art has been invariably upon the "tortures of the damned" and rarely upon the rewards of heaven.

Once death is understood, we can subconsciously shift the focus of our efforts toward taking full advantage of the opportunities this present incarnation presents. An incarnation becomes "a cycle" of potentials and opportunities, not simply "a life" of struggles, regrets and frustrations. We can cease doing that which will make our Bardo experience fearsome and we can focus our efforts toward liberation.

The ord "Bardo" is a Tibetan word that refers to the place we go between each incarnation. The Bardo begins just prior to the moment of actual death and lasts through the "forty-nine" states of awareness on the inner planes following death. There are also "forty-nine days" that represent an esoteric cycle of time, or cycles of experiences, or cycle degrees through which a Human passes. For the spiritually evolved soul, these "forty-nine days" may be passed through in but a few brief moments.

Forty-nine is the square of the sacred number seven. Scientifically, there are seven recognized degrees of light. Esoterically, there are seven degrees of *maya*, or illusion within the universe. There are seven globes in a planetary chain. There are seven rounds of evolution that a Human travels on a planetary chain, making up the forty-nine or seven-times-seven stations of active evolutionary existence.

According to ancient alchemists, the atomic structure of the whole vast phenomenal or lower Universe is based upon the mystical number seven, the seven-times-seven or forty-nine-frequencies. They relate in turn to the seven chemical phases of the Five Elements.

Humans have Seven Rounds of active existence. In the First Round of our planet the element Fire evolved. In the Second, the element Air separated from the Fire, resulting in an enclosure of the embryonic planet in a fire-air mist. In the Third Round, Air overpowering and abated some of the fiery element and produced the element Water.

The fourth Round, the Round in which the planet is in now, is presently evolving, the combined activity of Air and Water neutralizes the activity of Fire, creating a crust upon the surface and driving the element Fire toward the center of the planet, the crust becoming the element Earth.

During the Fifth, Sixth and Seventh Rounds, the Ether Element will be brought to its perfection. Out of its perfection will evolve two more elements, operating through the mind-consciousness. These latter two, not usually called elements, relate to mind and spirit. With the evolution of the Ether element, the waking consciousness will be able to absorb the memory records of all past experiences of the soul as it assumes transcendental consciousness. From transcendental consciousness, knowledge will proceed toward wisdom, and the Seventh Round will see Mastership for the Human species. Then the Divine Ether will descend like a heavenly dew to diffuse the mundane elements of our atmosphere.

How does this relate to the after-death Bardo experiences? Since the fifth element Ether, has not yet evolved for the Human race en masse, only those who have developed the very highest consciousness will be able to see and recognize the "Light Path of the Wisdom of Perfected Action," or THE CLEAR LIGHT. It reflects the highest aspect of Divine Mind, and the Human species has not yet unfolded innate spiritual attributes that would reflect or relate to this ultimate divinity.

The planet and its Human species, however, have passed the nadir, or low point, of involution in this present fourth Round, and are now in the upswing of evolution toward the Light of Source. Because of this, some souls will be ready for the ultimate initiation. Having overcome the darkness within at the moment of death, they will be able to see, THE

CLEAR LIGHT and the dawning of the Ether, element which delivers complete salvation.

In many of the Mysteries, especially the Hermetic, the initiation ceremony closely paralleled the seven states of the death Bardo experiences, all symbolizing the sevenfold elements of consciousness while in the psychic state immediately following death. The psychic states were symbolically labeled the *Forty-Nine Powers of the Mystery of the Seven Vowels*.

In these Mysteries, the Seven-Lettered Names of God who lead forth the souls at the time of death become liberated. During the initiation rites, the Christos leads the candidates for initiation to the feet of the Seven-Voweled God. There, at His feet, the initiate is given the "seven thunders uttered within the Seven Vowels" and the Secret Word, Sign, Grip and the knowledge of which will lead the Human into Liberation. Liberation from the Wheel of Birth and Death is the ultimate goal.

Those Humans who have studied the Mysteries will enter into THE CLEAR LIGHT during the Bardo. Others will merge with the Secondary Light, others the third aspect of Light. But during the forty-nine days or levels of consciousness, each soul will pass through the seven phases of involuntary-evolutionary processes.

In the maternal womb prior to physical birth, the fetus passes through the evolutionary organic structures from an amoeba-like cell to the perfected Human form. Also, at the time of death, the consciousness passes through similar "evolutionary" experiences, living again the memory created during incarnation, since the physical body is no more than a womb through which the spirit develops its potential.

At the time of death, the spirit emerges from the womb of the physical form with only the attributes it has developed while encased within that form. In the after-death state of Bardo, which is the embryonic state of the spirit in the astral or psychic World, the consciousness experiences the Bardo psychic conditions.

Just as the physical in its embryonic state within the physical womb passes from amoeba to Human, so does the consciousness pass through physical processes in its embryonic states within the Bardo, each soul "disembarking at the consciousness station" where they can best reside. If the Human fails to grasp THE CLEAR LIGHT, they will still be given forty-nine different opportunities of salvation and escape from rebirth.

Humans possess a seven-fold constitution; that is, seven principles of consciousness are integrated within each Human. Each of the seven is again composed of seven lesser degrees, the total composing Forty-nine Powers of the Mystery of the Seven Vowels. The forty-nine days of the Bardo clearly symbolize the stages or states of consciousness which erupt, each following the other, as the Human's seven principles of consciousness depart the vibratory wavelengths of Earth to become transmuted to a higher atomic frequency of the Otherworld. As the Human experiences the seven phases of consciousness-alterations, they are given forty-nine viewings of their idea of the Savior, their chosen Master, such as Jesus, Buddha, Siva, Vishnu, Zoroaster, or Mohammed; the teacher who warrants their highest love, reverence and respect by asking for guidance and protection they may, when recognized, lead the Human to liberation from their karma.

THE THREE PHASES OF THE BARDO

1. *PHASE ONE* (Chikhai Bardo)
   A. This is the dawning of THE CLEAR LIGHT which begins just prior to death and continues for about twenty minutes following the cessation of the breath. Its duration may be for the time it takes to snap a finger, a twinkling of an eye or for several days. For the average person, the usual time is about twenty minutes. If the person fails to merge with THE CLEAR LIGHT during the first twenty minutes of death, their consciousness wakens from this death swoon to experience--
   B. The Secondary Clear Light, which dawns immediately after death. The quality of the Secondary Clear Light will depend upon the measure of spiritual vibration developed with the person. Again, failure to maintain oneness within this Secondary Clear Light results in--

2. *PHASE TWO* (Chonyid Bardo)
   Karmic apparitions appear in this phase. The person views scenes of highest heavens as well as those of lower Worlds, forms and figures, according to the status of their own thought-world during their Earth life. Here again, if their inner darkness overshadows the lights and the benign figures and the scenes of heaven, then this phase, too, will pass and the person enters--

3. *PHASE THREE* (Sidpa Bardo)
>   This is the Lonesome Valley. In this gloomy twilight the benign hallucinatory visions vanish and the person becomes aware that they have departed Earth life. They understand that, even though their physical form is "dead," they, the real person is very much alive. They face now the thought forms of their negative emotions.

Even now, if they can remember to do so, they can call upon the name of their Savior image to gain help from On High. Most people are too distracted by the threatening shadows of seeming enemies, the roar of stormy winds and the sudden quiet and utter aloneness in the midst of a vast nothingness; but if they can recognize the unreality of it all and roll with the passing parade, their appeals and prayers can liberate them from the Lonesome Valley. If their karma prevents it, they descend to face the judgment.

THE SAVING GRACE OF THE CLEAR LIGHT (Part A of *PHASE ONE*)
The first stage of the Bardo, called *"the transitional state at the moment of death,"* heralds a dawning of THE CLEAR LIGHT. As the empiric consciousness of the objective World fades, the person may pass into what would be recognized as a kind of coma. It is not a descent into unconsciousness; rather it is uplifting into super consciousness, or the opening of the subjective mind upon THE CLEAR LIGHT.

THE CLEAR LIGHT is the reflection of consciousness devoid of all darkness, all limitations. It is that which is beyond all Human description since it possesses neither height, width, depth nor weight. It is Purified Perfection, shining like a dazzling sun upon the mirror of the mind as the consciousness passes from limitation of brain-bondage to expanded awareness at the moment of death. At this moment, the mind is like a mirror, and only when it is cleared of all karmic obstructions can the mind reflect THE CLEAR LIGHT.

The Void is not truly a void, because a void implies a center and circumference of nothingness. Our Void is described as a void because, again, such a state of pure consciousness is beyond description. It is like no other experiences in our World.

Since there is no name or color or form to give it, the Void seems to summarize its beingness, the Void having no width, depth, height, center, color nor name. We could call it *God*, because the words used to describe the Void also could describe God as the Supreme Being above all Human description. Actually, one would not be too far amiss to speak of THE CLEAR LIGHT as coming face to face with God.

The Void cannot be equated with Nirvana. The Void is consciousness free of all limitations, whereas Nirvana describes a state related to *sangsara* (the finite Worlds). In the Void, a person's consciousness, freed of all darkness and limitations, experiences Oneness with that which is beyond all consciousness. In such a state there is, momentarily, no time, no space, no emotions, nor action.

There is only Being-in-Bliss. Those who are able to remain united at-one-ment with THE CLEAR LIGHT can experience deathbed salvation. They have gained liberation from their karma, having broken the cyclic rhythm to the Wheel of Birth and Death, and need go no further from the higher dimensions.

For such a one, there will be no confrontation with the hallucinatory beings, either beneficent or malevolent. Merging with THE CLEAR LIGHT, the person travels no Lonesome Valley, nor do they endure the scenes of the judgment. They are liberated from the pathway of normal evolution. Such liberation seldom comes to the souls who have not prepared themselves while living for the ultimate experience of consciousness expansion; nor does it come to the souls involved in the karmic penalties of an evil life.

To be liberated one must prepare to give up their self to become their true Self, which can feel like annihilating one's known self. Immersion in THE CLEAR LIGHT is only immersion of the low self into the High Self. One must come to know that such an event does not mean annihilation, loss of contact with loved ones, cessation of the personality as who we were; it means that we become more.

THE SECONDARY CLEAR LIGHT (Part B of *PHASE ONE*)

If a person's consciousness is clouded with the fog of karma, the person fails to observe the first dawning of THE CLEAR LIGHT; they have a second opportunity in the first stage of the Bardo. As the first of THE CLEAR LIGHT fades away unobserved by the departing because its dazzling brightness is beyond the person's perception, there dawns a Secondary Clear Light, still dazzling in its brightness but dimmed considerably from the brightness of THE CLEAR LIGHT.

It may be that the perception of the person can behold this Secondary Clear Light, can enter it and can find their place of harmony therein. They may feel the actual biological processes occurring in the depths of their being, the heat rising kundalini, the electromagnetic power of the chakras as they respond to the newly released psychic force.

The person may see flashing radiances of colors and lights and hear churning; swishing sounds of energy forces being set in motion in the new form, so sensitive is the person to a new dimension of being. The person may be torn between two decisions: should they relax and float back into the dazzling CLEAR LIGHT that keeps intermittently dawning before them, or should they delight in practicing the powers of their newly opened psychic senses?

Much of the person's after-death awareness will depend upon how the person responds to the confusing alternatives which now open before them. Clearly, a person should not center their attention upon the Secondary Clear Light but, in a state of repose, drift with the psychic currents back toward THE CLEAR LIGHT.

At this stage, even a trained mystic could easily become distracted. One should ride the tides of the experience, not attempting to direct or assist the processes. It is important at this point for one to concentrate upon their chosen Master, such as Jesus, Buddha, Siva, Vishnu, Zoroaster, or Mohammed, the teacher who warrants their highest love, reverence and respect asking for guidance and protection.

PHASE TWO: CHONYID BARDO

With the dawning of the Second Phase, the person is now completely freed from the physical form. Their intellect is expanded and they are awakened. With the departure of the physical waking consciousness, they will experience a psychic thrill which heralds a further opening of spiritual consciousness into a state of lucidity. This is called *the transitional state of reality*.

THE GUIDING FORCE OF KARMA

During the Human's entire journey through the Bardo, karma will be the guiding force of destiny. It may be the person's karmic lot to gain liberation in the first phase of the Bardo by recognizing and merging with THE CLEAR LIGHT. And in this case, the Human may not experience the death trance at all but, recognizing THE CLEAR LIGHT just prior to death, may step out of the body in full consciousness, entering God's White Light.

Accomplishing this, a person will be completely liberated from the Wheel of Birth and Death. If and when the person seeks rebirth, it will be due to their own desires and they will be born in full consciousness of their life on the inner planes and their previous lives, returning to Earth to accomplish a spiritual mission.

If it is not the person's karmic lot to gain liberation in the first phase, they will proceed through the Bardo, departing it at whatever stage their karma allows. They will be given other opportunities to recognize the symbolic "Saviors" and if they can perceive them, they may recognize and accept them.

If a person, because of a karmically clouded consciousness, recognizes no Light and no Savior, they will proceed strictly according to their karma and may depart the Bardo to enter a lower vibratory plane on the Other side.

If during their life the person has become a disciple and turned toward the higher Path, the deities, Saviors of the Bardo, assume a different aspect. Through these thought forms the disciple will be inseparably related to great beings on the inner planes.

Sangsara is a Sanskrit word which has no English equivalent. Among its meanings are:

1. Existence in the finite Worlds of matter
2. Ceaseless wandering back and forth between the World of Human incarnation and the Otherworld
3. Attachment to things of Earth and responding to the down-pulling desires of life in Human form which draw the thoughts constantly Earthward after one reaches the inner planes, resulting in
4. Reincarnation

All these woven together constitute what Tibetans call "*sangsara,*" the area of existence in which the soul is caught upon the Wheel of Birth and Death. *Sangsara*, for some souls, extends beyond Earth life to include the astral and even the lower mental Worlds.

One is liberated from sangsara when they are finally liberated from the Wheel of Birth and Death; when their karma no longer requires them to incarnate in Human form. Only when karmic sins are overcome is the soul released from *sangsara*.

Understanding *sangsara* and the soul's liberation from it is an important part of understanding the Bardo, and the science of dying. The state of Nirvana is the opposite to that of *sangsara*. *Sangsara* is being caught in the web of Earth existence; Nirvana, to use the Sanskrit meaning, is "blowing out" the illusory, unreal reflection of physical existence to see by the Divine Light of spiritual existence.

PHASE THREE: SIDPA BARDO

The great masses of Humanity will recognize neither THE CLEAR LIGHT nor the Secondary Clear Light. They will never even have heard of them and those untrained to recognize the actual Second Phase will merge into the Sidpa Bardo, the Third Stage, called by the Tibetans the *transitional state while seeking rebirth*.

In this instance, the word "rebirth" does not apply to reincarnation but it means the time of "awakening" from the Bardo and emerging to ascend or descend to the vibratory level of astral life most harmonious to one's inner soul development.

In the seven zones of the Sidpa, the soul faces the personified build-up of thought forms associated with certain negative emotions expressed during their recent incarnation. In each zone of experience, the emotions erupt into seven degrees of manifestation. In one zone, the person could face the thought forms containing the total result of their expressions of anger, their self-created thought forms of jealousy; of lust; of greed; of hatred. One will discover their attachment to carnal desires.

16.

The Judgment

We do not escape our karma. In the Bardo, if we miss merging with THE CLEAR LIGHT or THE SECONDARY CLEAR LIGHT we will meet everyone we have wronged on Earth in the Bardo drama-visions and will vicariously suffer their sufferings, their anguish. We will confront those who have wronged us and face the test of forgiveness. Here, rather than ourselves, our soul judges us according to how we respond to these visions. We are tested to see how well we respond to the initiation of our karma.

If we fail the tests by holding onto any hatred, revenge or carnal lust, we will exit the Bardo and move to one of the lower spiritual planes possibly the lower astral plane. If we respond well to these tests, forgiving our enemies, turning away from carnality, we will emerge from the judgment redeemed and will be taken to a place in the higher spiritual spheres.

DEATHBED REPENTANCE

The living can contribute a great deal toward helping the dying person by guiding the consciousness, through suggestion, out of its vague drifting and directing it to concentrate on the approaching Light. Death trauma can influence one's life in the Otherworld.

While it is true that one can experience deathbed "salvation," which means avoiding the Bardo, it can never be wholly accomplished unless the departing is aware that THE CLEAR LIGHT will dawn, and the dying person recognizes it for what it means. Although masses, extreme unction and prayers are effective, the last rites become acutely enhanced through knowledge of the secrets of initiation into THE CLEAR LIGHT.

Any ceremony may lend succor and strength as one passes through the swoon of death, but unless one recognizes THE CLEAR LIGHT and takes full advantage of the opportunity to merge with it, they cannot gain complete liberation from their karmic sins. Liberation from karma is what is actually meant by the Christian's "salvation," though the Christians call it "being saved from sin."

A deathbed ritual, ignorantly performed, could be of dubious benefit. A Christian, having been taught the "value" of deathbed repentance, often will recall and hold vividly a memory of all their sins, orally or mentally. This is a dreadful mistake. One should never enter the Otherworld immersed in thoughts of past misdeeds. One should strive to enter the Otherworld immersed only in THE CLEAR LIGHT.

The proper procedure would be to repent and seek forgiveness long before the deathbed. To remember these past sins and negative memories at the time of passing can cause negative memories to appear in vivid reality in the Bardo. A sincere confession and prayer for forgiveness is good only if the person can forget the wrong acts and push thoughts of sins and negativity far into the background, replacing them with an aura of God's Pure White Light.

Regardless of how many masses or prayers are said, the only thing that can destroy the karmic record of sins and misdeeds is the essence of White Light, whether it be THE CLEAR LIGHT of the Bardo, the Secondary Clear Light or any of the Lesser Lights; all are portions of God's Pure White Light. The only possible way to overcome karma at the time of death is to recognize THE CLEAR LIGHT when it dawns, and to strive to hold to it with every ounce of will and wisdom.

God's Pure White Light appears regardless of the religious affiliation of the person. God's Pure White Light is what Christians call the "saving blood," and it alone can "wipe away all stains of sin," whether it be for the Christian, Jew, Moslem, Hindu, Buddhist, Zoroastrian, Gnostic or atheist.

Jesus said: *"I am the Way, the Truth and the Light, and no man cometh unto the Father but by me."* (John 14:6) He did not necessarily mean through His own intervention as a personal being, but through the Clear Christ Light of Truth that He represented.

Looking to a priest, minister or rabbi to absolve one's sin is not enough, for seldom do they know how to purge the karmic record of the individual with THE CLEAR LIGHT. The priest's solemnly intoned words carry little or no causative power of absolution unless they direct the dying person toward personal involvement in THE CLEAR LIGHT; nor is it enough simply to confess repentance.

Christians are sometimes taught that, regardless of how evil a life one leads, simply by a personal act of repentance at the moment of death, one is assured release from punishment and awarded a place in paradise. This does not mean that there is no such thing as being "saved by grace." The error lies in teaching Humans that the choice lies with them. It does not. A person may truly repent on their deathbed, gain a soul-clearing and, thereby, enter fully into THE CLEAR LIGHT and be "saved", but whether or not they are exempt from their just karma is not their choice. A person should repent because they experience a deep and sincere remorse, not because they hope to escape punishment.

It is very misleading to teach that one can disregard Divine Law all one's Earthly life and hope for deathbed salvation simply by "accepting Jesus as one's personal Savior." Everything will depend upon recognition of THE CLEAR LIGHT when it dawns in the first phase of death. THE CLEAR LIGHT is God's "saving grace."

God-realization is open to attainment every hour of every day, yet how few pause to discover it. Such an attainment is doubly difficult at the awesome moment of death unless one has been taught and trained to grasp THE CLEAR LIGHT. The first dawning of THE CLEAR LIGHT is dazzling and radiantly bright. Each sighting thereafter will see THE CLEAR LIGHT diminished until it is reduced to the measure of Light within the consciousness of the person dying. The Light of the Bardo with which the soul finally merges will be in exact ratio to the Light within the person's own consciousness. It is this merging with the Bardo Light that determines the atomic structure of the new astral body.

For the very good and the very bad, THE CLEAR LIGHT may appear only as a quick flash of light, like the snap of the fingers. The very good with a prior knowledge of the saints, having seen it before in their prayers or meditations and recognizing it for what it is, will merge with it instantly and be carried to a high vibrational plane. The personality, at the moment of death, will merge with the degree of Light the person is able to perceive and absorb into their consciousness.

Masses and prayers said for the repose of the souls of the departed are important. In their new life, the person is conscious of these actions and derives help energetically from the prayers. They feel the energy and intent of the prayers of those still in body on Earth.

Many are helped to adjust to their new surroundings, especially those who emerge from the Bardo to find themselves in purgatory. Purgatory is, in a sense, only another word for an extended Bardo, a time of purging, of purification. The most certain way to avoid spending a trying period in purgatory is to enter the Otherworld with a full faith in immortality, knowing with certainty that the soul has the power to create its own conditions.

Death is a spiritual initiation, not just liberation of the soul from the limitation of the mind from its waking consciousness limitations. The length of time in the Bardo depends upon the spiritual status of the soul.

The entire purpose of the Bardo experience is to reveal to a person the exact karmic results of his past incarnation, the impact of which, saturating the subconscious, remains forever with one through their journey in Otherworld regions and into their next incarnation.

Each incident of death and each journey through the Bardo points a person toward a higher state of awareness in their next embodiment. Never does one forget completely the experiences in the Bardo and, after reincarnating, when the voice of conscience rises to warn a person to beware of some wrong doing, it is the subconscious mind bringing to remembrance the past Bardo experience.

The conscience, then, is nothing more than a subconscious recall of the last Bardo experienced before the present incarnation. It is the haunting of one's own thought forms rising to guide and warn the soul as one travels the next Human incarnation.

No specific rules can be given concerning what may confront an individual in their own Bardo, for the after-death experiences are the most individualized that anyone is ever called upon to meet. Every Bardo experience will differ according to the individual's own mental content. An ardent Christian may meet the Master Jesus, dimly or vividly, according to their own personal concept of the image of a Savior. The mentally created image can be directly connected with the Christ himself from the higher planes, thereby becoming enhanced far beyond that of the usual Bardo deity. People who follow other religions will see other deities.

In summary, we build our own Bardo battles, and the thought forms with which we wrestle become symbols of our guilt, our hatreds, our greed's, jealousies, envies, egos and passions. They are real only to the degree that we bestow force and power upon and within them. Once on the threshold of the Bardo, we will meet the self-created thought forms of our enemies, our loved ones and our worshipped deities.

Once the newly released power of the kundalini, with its heat and light-producing phenomena, has subsided, a lower form of creative energy begins to rise from the generative organs up the spine of the astral form.

At this point the person has not yet actually awakened to astral life. While undergoing the Bardo, the person is still in the process of "dying." One is in the "labor" of spiritual birth.

Only souls who are extremely carnal will experience the final phases of Sidpa, and only the degenerates will face the final judgment.

If we listen intently to our conscience and follow its suggestions, our next death and Bardo experience will be a time of delight and an opportunity to attain supreme liberation.

17.

Borderland, Highland, Midland

Borderland is one of the first levels of the Astral Plane. Many, entering Borderland utterly ignorant of its presence and its laws, require enlightenment to grasp that they are dead. Once they do, they are filled with terror lest they be plunged into "the outer darkness," or sent to the blazing depths of torment. These misguided ones need to be gradually led into the light. They are called "the sleepers." They are the souls who, during Earth life, became strongly convinced that after death they would sleep for millenniums until the great Day of Judgment. They will not accept that their death-sleep has been of short duration. They are convinced that thousands of years must have come and gone. Many believe so firmly they actually pass into a brief state of slumber. While they remain asleep they can be reached with teachings and suggestions before their sleep automatically terminates.

At the time of their rousing to full consciousness, responding to the soul call, the sleepers leave the shadowy valley of rest to take up life on the astral. We shall not all sleep, but we will be changed.

The few who spend extended lengths of time in sleep are:
1. Those who experienced lingering illness which exhausts the soul as well as the body;
2. Those who have left behind loved ones whose uncontrollable grief creates unnecessary pain for the newly arrived Human;
3. Those who feel a strong desire to continue life in the body; who experience their greatest attraction earthward and thus find adjustment difficult.

Even for these, sleep is not long. The time is spent in the presences of those who know how to heal through reaching the subconscious mind and assisting these people toward adjustment.

LIGHT ON OTHER PLANES

Earth Humans conceive of light simply as the opposite of darkness. Its vibrational qualities are not important. Darkness, to Humans, means a lack of certain vibrations by which the retina of the eye registers the presence of external things.

The same is true of the Astral. Those in the dimmer regions are those who lack the sight-sense faculty to perceive certain vibrations. With the development of these spiritual faculties, that which was invisible becomes visible. There is a definite vibratory relationship between a spirit and that spirit's environment.

Borderlanders see Earth Humans only through a mist. Only those who turn their attention earthward to serve Humans they have left behind will learn to focus their sight to clearly discern Earth scenes. They must learn how to adjust their vision to accommodate the light of Earth. They "see" the spiritual body much more clearly than the physical. When they speak to Humans they speak to the inner spiritual ear, but they can hear Earth's sound and can even discern thoughts, since thoughts are of the spirit.

Borderlanders find joy in performing missions to Earth, though such missions are frequently more difficult for them than Highlanders. When they touch a Human, they touch the spiritual form. Only the most sensitive are aware of it. And only the trained Human hears their voices speaking to the spiritual ear. They are "heard" a great deal more often than is realized; however, not as physical sounds but as subtle mental impressions.

As one progresses higher, sight perception adjusts to sustain with ease the prevailing degree of light. When one adjusts from Highland to Summerland it will require a while for their visual perception to accommodate itself to the higher frequency of light. Once this is accomplished, when they make return visits to Highland they find it dimmed and must adjust their sight-sense accordingly.

Such an adjustment is fairly simple. However, journey into Midland, Borderland and Earth itself requires considerable adjustment, as each plane's darkness increases as one moves downward. Humans who radiate a light about themselves are easily seen and contacted, whereas those whose auras are dark are difficult to perceive.

If Etherians from higher spheres did not possess higher intuitive faculties than those of sight, it would prove exceedingly difficult for them to approach Earth and to aid Humans with dark auras. But they do possess extrasensory powers and discernment. When Etherians from higher planes descend to Borderland, they are invisible to the inhabitants unless they desire to be seen. They have the power to make themselves visible whenever they desire to do so. Even so, some see them better than others.

If Borderlanders journey too far into higher, brighter realms before their time of graduation, they experience an exhaustion of life force which forces a retreat to the Lowlands. Some can penetrate farther than others. Some also see into the light better than others, discerning the beings, scenes and glory awaiting their graduation.

Borderland is filled with those who remain attracted to Earth. They made little spiritual progress during incarnation. They are not wholly bad. Rather, they are the vacillating, aimless souls who frittered away their opportunities and made no use of them. Or they may be restrained from ascending by affection for their loved ones and an affinity for their pursuits. Thus they prefer to remain near the Earth sphere.

In addition, there are the younger souls whose spiritual education is still unfinished. They are in the course of elementary training. And there are those who have been incarnated in imperfect bodies and still have to learn what they should have learned on Earth. There are those too who have prematurely departed Earth and, through no fault of their own, still have much to learn before they can progress.

The average newcomer dwells a while in the Midlands of the Astral, bypassing Borderland but pausing before entering the brighter Highlands. Many remain in Highland before moving onto Summerland since Highland is nearer Earth and their loved ones there.

Mortals build their first home in Etheria (the spirit world) largely by acts and deeds performed while on Earth. The silent work of construction begins during early youth, and is continued during one's mortal life, each act producing a corresponding effect upon the structure.

Earth Humans seldom realize that they are the unconscious architects and builders of the first homes they will occupy over there. The wrongdoings of mortal life mar and tarnish their beauty, and each spiritual thought and activity adds to them. Indeed the works of mortals precede them to the world of spirit.

HOMES AND BUILDINGS IN BORDERLAND

Often homes in Borderland include a series of houses grouped together, representing a temporary educational center rather than an actual home. Each inhabitant is taught how to best serve others, much as Humans are trained in a trade on Earth.

They progress from one house to another in the compound as they acquire knowledge. Only after they graduate do they depart for their real home. In the interim all is not training, to be sure. Rather, much of their training is in the form of happy excursions abroad in the new life, learning the relationship and kinship of all life.

They observe that although trees and landscapes are similar to those of Earth, still there is responsiveness to the buildings, to the birds, even to the people, that is not apparent on Earth. Each individual's mental atmosphere has a unique effect upon clothing. Although all Humans in any certain "home" wear clothing of similar quality and texture, the colors and hues are modified according to individual character.

FACSIMILIES OF EARTHLY HOMES AND CITIES

In the city of Los Angeles there are beautiful homes, gardens, lakes, slums and undesirable districts, all coagulated to form a metropolis? There is a facsimile of Los Angeles in the zones of Borderland, interpenetrating and overshadowing the Earth city. This Borderland city has its spots of ugliness, slums, and undesirable districts and well as average dwellings, neither beautiful nor ugly.

Superimposing the Borderland city, there is a third city residing on the Midland Plane of the astral. In this city there are only beautiful vistas. There are no slum counterparts, for those who dwell there have risen above the kind of life which would create slums and ugliness.

So long as Humans live and think undesirable thoughts and habits, there must inevitably remain undesirable areas to which they gravitate in Borderland. When Earth Humans have risen mentally and spiritually above such habits, the corresponding areas on the lower spiritual spheres will cease to be.

Another version of Los Angeles in Highland is situated over the Borderland and Midland Los Angeles, each city becomes more spacious than the other, more beautiful, more purified, more ethereal.

HOMES IN MIDLAND

Humans should fill their Earth lives with good deeds, should bear with courage their belief in eternal life, and speak fully of their convictions, lest by failing to do so and shrinking from criticism one looks back from Over there with stinging remorse for having lost such golden opportunities.

Homes in Etheria reflect the character of those indwelling them. Although fairly permanent, they are quickly modified according to the wishes of the occupant. Time has no effect on buildings. They neither crumble nor decay. Their duration depends completely upon the will of those who created them. They need not be demolished to be modified, but structural changes may be made while buildings stand.

Thought is spirit substance in motion. An idea, on the other hand, is a static form of spirit substance possessing the quality of endurance principles. Every spiritual plane object is the expression of some thought. Every bird, tree, landscape, home, temple, is the result of some action of mind upon particle composing the atmosphere.

Houses and gardens and organic life of every variety become filled with the spirit. A spirit may acquire that which they are capable of mentally visualizing. Such power is gained only as one becomes accustomed to the laws of the spirit spheres. Whether one inhabits a hovel or a mansion in the higher spheres, one's home surroundings reflects the individual's individuality as a mirror reflects physical appearance.

A Human on Earth chooses their home according to their means and circumstances. But in the world of spirit they are surrounded by, and reflect, a picture of that which they are. A Human who is poor in spirit finds themselves corresponding in poverty in their environment. Every act of kindness, compassion, love, mercy, beneficence, results in the greater beautification of the home or landscape.

Mansions in Midland are sometimes the exact home that the person dreamed of possessing while on Earth. If one analyzes themselves spiritually they may come to understand that which they will inhabit in their afterlife state. In such mansions there are rooms in which they entertain friends. Other apartments are dedicated to hours of study, and again there is a chamber apart, sheltered from every eye, where one withdraws to be utterly alone. Such moments may not be shared even by their loved ones.

This room is reserved for the person contemplating their inner life, when they desire to commune with those on higher planes to work on their spiritual evolution.

In such homes there is always cleanliness, for dust and dirt have no part in such beauty. There are no noxious insects, including odors, or thieves. These estates open out onto the landscape itself. Any enclosures are not to shelter one from the environment, for why would one shelter themselves from heaven? Enclosures are simply for personal comfort or occasional withdrawing from others.

Many rooms in such homes have one complete side open to the air and landscapes. The roof, transparent and of prismatic hues, is often supported by columns entwined with flowing vines.

In these dimensions homes are created by thought. On Earth homes are created by thought, but with the difference that on Earth one thinks out the plan of a home, employs an architect who draws the plan on the flat dimensions of paper. After the plan is completed as blueprint, the builder and his workers construct the home of Earth's materials.

On the astral, Humans also think out the plan for their homes, then build them of the substance of Etheria, the "matter" of this plane being so tenuous that it can be molded by the action of the mind. If one need bricks over there, one fashions them from the etheric matter.

HOMES IN HIGHLAND

Among the buildings are huge open air pavilions where meetings are frequently held. Some are reserved for religious service, while others house festive occasions. Some are topped by huge domes resting on tall pillars. The temples contain altars and display spiritual symbols, while the pavilions of festivities are filled with colorful lights, chairs, benches, in formal profusion.

There are great buildings resembling Greek temples, with high arches, porticos and many flights of stairs. Many are circular with vast rotundas richly embossed with gems of myriad colors hung with drapes of silken textures and topped with domes of semi-opaque stones which reflect in pouring softened light.

In every building color is blended with harmonious colors. In some the effect is exhilarating; in others, tranquilizing. Precious jewels, metals, ornaments, pedestals, hanging of shimmering materials are common. From rooftops observers look into vast glories of higher lands, or enjoy the lakes, woodlands, flowers, rolling hills of one's own sphere in Highland.

Around many buildings there hangs a golden mist, not one that obscures but rather bathes the atmosphere in heavenly perfume. There are faint blues, pinks, purples, and gold blending in amazing tones. Each building has its own dominant tint and musical background, its own quality, according to its indwelling resident.

Often vast plains extend beyond cities. Just as tourists group together to visit foreign lands on Earth, so do these spirits. Some are organized as companies of beings, learning lessons through excursions as well as simply viewing their new world. Others are teachers experimenting with spiritual forces. Many are companies of friends joining together to visit other friends. Travelers are never unwelcome. Those arriving from higher planes are greeted with amazing pageants. Festive parties are numerous. Not like the sordid "parties" familiar on Earth where intoxicants measure the merriment, these are filled with music and laughter.

Visitors from higher planes always arrive with serious purposes and teach of their lives in homes in brighter spheres. Frequently they are on a mission to the Lowlands. They impart blessings to the inhabitants of each level they travel through.

Travel is often by aerial flight, sometimes via the slower method of walking. Shrines are frequent along such highways and resting havens as well with fountains filled with prana-filled waters.

The lakes around which cities are built are busy with boating excursions, and it is by this method that visitors often arrive, frequently coming from vast distance. Great mansions grace the lakeshores. There are countless wooded areas, not wild nor unkempt but abounding in wild flowers and birds with colorful plumage. Statues, shrines, summerhouses, benches, pathways, magnificent trees, flowering vines, musical brooks, and green glades abound. From rising hilltops other cities may be seen, gleaming like diamonds in the distance.

There are spaces of ground paved with alabaster, appearing much as a flooring of flaming glass, not as flames of Earth but of moving, flickering rays of light and shadow. Some buildings are busy communication centers, receiving messages from all spheres, both lower and higher, and dispensing them according to their destination, or acting upon them if services are asked, points of coordinating and expatiating as required.

Many roof domes seem to be of crystal, the better to diffuse rays of light into halls and rooms. On the walls in some homes pictures are hung that slowly change under one's concentrated scrutiny. They are reflecting scenes occurring on other planes. Some depict scenes on Earth; others reflect ceremonies being performed on higher planes.

One finds themselves, when they finally depart Earth, in a hotel or a palace, depending on the spiritual record they write while on Earth.

Homes, like garments, are fashioned from "solidified" thought substance. Some are more substantial than others, being created of more powerful thought force.

Thought is the creative force of all things, whether here or there. All worlds, universes, suns, moons and stars were created by thought. Such thought creativity is beyond our conception now, but when thought operates at its highest potential, it becomes tangible substance. Under the impact of thought force, such substance can also melt away.

THE SINGING WATERS

There are singing waters there, which are not waters at all, although they flow much like a stream on Earth. Immersion in them brings an indescribable sense of rejuvenation. They possess no wetness but are filled with a life force that renews and invigorates the cells of the new form. They are more like a ray of light than a liquid substance. These "rivers of life" are to be found in abundance. Strollers often wade fully clothed through brooks just to absorb their electrifying energies.

There are fountains of these living waters in almost every home in Midland and in the upper spheres. The fountain itself seems to be composed of the "family gems." That is, if the inhabitant habitually wears a blue gem in ornamenting his or her hair or in the garments or girdle worn, the same color will be carried out in the fountain before their home. Though colors fluctuate, one certain color will predominate. Even the water itself rising from the fountains displays the same hue. As the waters rise and fall they seem to emit actual musical tones. To stand under a spray of this water-like substance is to experience a most exhilarating sensation. The dewy moisture that remains quickly evaporates, leaving the clothing not only dry but also with a sparkling surface.

NOMADS

Some higher plane Etherians choose to carry their "home" with them. That is, they require no fixed habitation, preferring to roam at will where challenges can be found and where there are spiritual missions to accomplish, much as Jesus did while on Earth.

Just as in Earth life, whatever is necessary is obtainable, but methods of attainment differ. To whatever plane a person is magnetically attracted, the matter of that plane is subject to the control of their will. But only to the degree that they have developed will power. All that they desire is immediately subservient to their wishes, if they can mold the matter to their desires.

A home over there is truly "a home not made with hands." But to attain all that one desires it becomes imperative that they develop spiritual power that they may have neglected while on Earth. It is only then that one usually comes to the full realization of how poor in spirit they truly are, and they feel remorse that they so neglected spiritual schooling and the enfoldment of spiritual perception. One's objective life over there is gauged by the quality of their subjective perception and powers.

FLOWERS

You marvel at the beauty surrounding you and long to return to Earth to bring enlightenment to those left behind. There is much more for us to learn before we can speak to Humans on Earth with wisdom, and communicating is far more difficult than it would seem.

We are told flowers, as with all else, never die. If flowers never die what need is there for continued creating of more? Nothing is ever wasted in Etheria. Old flowers never die, they just fade away. They actually never become old, but when different floral arrangements are desired, previous bouquets simply vanish. The essence of which they are composed returns to its source. All things are living. There are no inanimate objects. Gardens continue as they are created unless someone changes their mind and mentally creates a change. There are no weeds and no changing of seasons or invading insects.

In Etheria flowers are not merely to be seen. They serve a vital purpose in that life force itself is exuded from them. One who strolls near a flower bed immediately is the stronger for it, since their entire aura may be penetrated by the out flowing life essence. Nor can a gardener impart it. This addition must come from Source. It is the Source that fills the flowers, the waters and the entire landscape with a vital life essence.

Birds abound here, more numerous than on Earth, and their plumage is far more colorful. The birds flash through the trees like streaks of gold and silver interlaced with vivid blues and reds, more radiant than anything found on Earth.

CITIES

As on Earth, many people prefer city living to homes in country estates. They congregate in closer communion. It is usually in the cities where the Halls of Learning are located, though not in congested areas. Buildings occupy large tracts of land even in the midst of cities, not to provide "parking space" but to be surrounded by spacious grounds and gardens.

No city on Earth compares with cities in Midland or Summerland. Cities are not centers of industry, smoke, traffic or crowds. They are simply a cluster of certain buildings, each surrounded by gardens, pools, walkways, benches, magnificent trees and rest areas. Usually a city is planned to diverge outward from a hub, much like a wheel, with broad thoroughfares leading toward a central building.

This central building could be called a Temple of the Seven Spheres, a church of all faiths. The separate faiths are not practiced once in Heaven; rather, these sanctuaries are places of meditation where the saints and the Source are honored.

These large centers are areas where groups gather to worship the Source of all Creation. The saints and higher vibrational teachers also come from higher spheres from time to time to speak of life where they live and the spiritual laws pertaining to their planes, or to impart blessings.

Spreading outward from this center are buildings devoted to learning various arts. These Halls of Learning serve all those dwelling in the outlying community as well as the city. Each city is composed of its own centers of learning and each serves the residents of its sphere. Among the schools are the hall of fabrics, the universities of the arts such as painting, sculpturing, lithography, metallurgy; the colleges of literature, of science, of music, of designing.

Over all there abides a sense of unity, of love, of oneness, for each city houses only those equally evolved, though not all are endowed with the same degree of character qualities. Some may need further development of patience, control of temper, greed, or jealousy; yet all have attained an equal level of soul evolvement. Love must be adapted to the wisdom of the personalities involved.

18.

Hell, Purgatory and Highland Hell and the Law of Retribution

Our soul is the architect of the body we inhabit. It did the best it could with the materials we provided. The next form we inhabit will be constructed from the materials we make available to the soul during this incarnation.

We contribute to the creation of our bodies and the circumstances into which we are born according to our karma. There is not one hell, there are many and each is created according to the one who makes it, for each person creates their own afterlife. The planes of "outer darkness" are not described here to frighten you, but it is useless to speak of the celestial realms if one dares not become aware of the whole truth. There are planes of darkness. It is well not to dwell too long upon this unpleasant aspect, but it is gratifying to know that the inhabitants of these regions no longer number among the billions. Humanity, entering the upward arc of its evolutionary cycle, no longer enters hell en masse.

In the early days of Earth's evolution, its lower astral regions were peopled by vast migrations of souls coming and going in rapid incarnations. With the passing eons, masses of Humanity, having experienced death and the Bardo many times, have perfected their astral forms and subconsciously learned many lessons. Thus, the vast surging masses of souls now congregate on the mid plane of the astral in the afterlife. Only the degenerate sinks to the lower levels.

Hell means various things to various people. Some never think of it at all. Others, when they do, believe that it applies only to other people. Some think they experience their portion of hell here on Earth, and that the afterlife cannot possibly be worse. Others believe that life has cheated them dreadfully, that they are victims of their enemies, and have arrived at their state of misery through no fault of their own.

Others believe that every individual creates their own environment, be it heavenly or hellish and, according to their level of consciousness, they experience misery or delight, or some state in between, right here on Earth, and that is true.

Hell is both a state of consciousness and a locality. In the Otherworld, hell is a place of self-made misery, a place one enters due to their own self-created anomalies. Always the miseries endured are related directly and indirectly to the miseries one inflicts on others. Never does a soul endure an unjust punishment. Somewhere, back in time, they have been the author of an equal injustice toward a fellow being.

This hellish condition, this misery, is not so much a punishment as a leveling of debts. It is not that God would "get even" for what one has done to others. It is simply that we are to be purified before we are capable of entering more heavenly regions.

Since such miseries are the natural results of one's own conduct, we must learn to regard our self-created hell as disguised progress, as "growing pains." We cannot "grow forward" until past debts are erased. Such leveling is necessary to our soul's enlightenment. Thus souls temporarily "go to hell" that they might someday "go to heaven."

WHERE IS HELL

In the ethers overshadowing the slum areas of every city on Earth, there exists a facsimile on the etheric plane. Rising above the slums of Los Angeles, Chicago, New York, London, Tokyo, Moscow as well as every slum district of every other city are found etheric hells on the inner planes.

No one planned their being there. No one charted a definite location. These regions exist simply because those in the hell regions of Earth have, through their dark emanations, actions and thoughts, created the facsimile on the astral. And to these locations gravitate the spirits who harmonize with the vibrations of such localities.

There a spirit stays until it comes to realize that its own unworthiness has caused it to be there and that it can rise only as it self-builds thoughts worthy of higher planes. It may require a long time. Since the soul lives forever, one has eternity in which to find repentance.

These regions are like submersion in a black muddy soup of smog. There, monstrous forms of Human beings reside in the very lowest state of degradation and solitude. Their bodies have acclimated to the darkness and the abominable stench of hatred. The fires of these awful regions are created by the burning rages which pour from the inhabitants as they continually walk about cursing God and Humans.

Other regions are filled with black, slimy, crawling things, perpetually advancing like an unending army of wet spiders and slithering eels. Very much like the hallucinations of a person experiencing the DT's. Only souls on the very lowest scale of Humanity will sink to these levels. They are fit only for those who, while on Earth, murdered for the sheer sadistic pleasure of giving pain to others; who hated with such abiding passion that they allowed the flames to consume any prospects for light. Their thoughts, giving vent to such blackness, surrounded their entire being with an emanation which drew them to the depths with which such conditions harmonize.

In this sense a soul does not go to hell. Rather, it is hell that goes into the Human. During a soul's stay in the darkness, the faces and forms of those they have wronged may continually rise before them, haunting, accusing, reminding them of their actions. One comes face-to-face with their true self. The thoughts of moral cowardice, false pretences, selfish motives, all have created thought forms that become part of their abode in this place of soul-revelation.

Guilt increases. In their frenzy to escape, they may choose many upward paths, only to find they must retreat. The cosmic forces which are the source of joy for others become a source of pain for them. No one forces them to remain in the gloom. They will choose to do just as they did while on Earth because they fitted themselves by deeds and thoughts to a darkened aura. For their own comfort, they must remain in the realm most harmonious with their inner darkness. They can eventually work themselves out of their condition through prayer and service to others. Hell is never an eternal place, and one's ascent into light is as rapid as they themselves can accomplish it.

How long the degenerate is left in these outer regions only they can tell; although they may be unaware of it, a guardian on a higher plane is always waiting and hoping for a word, a glimmer of remorse, contrition or self-blame; for a plea, for an opportunity to make good their wrong. Contemplating the wretchedness of the situation, eventually the time arrives when they begin to consider their awful fare and wonder how they might escape.

When they finally accept that they can no longer endure their torture and solitude and realize they may have been the cause of their situation, their thoughts may turn to asking for help. At that moment the Angel guardian will begin to help by sending light. Little by little the person finds themselves emerging from darkness into the twilight zones.

Often the degenerate finally realizes that they are the only one who can bring an end to their torment. Some refuse to relinquish their desires. In any case, there is not eternal punishment. For those who overcome, there is ultimate liberation from the lower regions. For those who persistently refuse such liberation, there is the ultimate return of the soul to another more difficult incarnation on Earth.

The soul on the lower realms is constantly reminded that there is a higher plane, is shown visions of what life could be like, and will be like, once they repent or change their mind. Just knowing what happiness others are enjoying is a great punishment, for they are quick to realize what might have been.

Only when they finally accept the knowledge that only they can free themselves by a change of attitude, only then do they begin to overcome their hatreds and learn the law of love.

SITUATIONS TO AVOID

There are those on the lower astral who vicariously continue bestial habits formed on Earth. Many drunkards who haunted saloons on Earth will still haunt them after taking up life on the astral. Some drunkards arriving on the inner planes do not repent and reform instead they gravitate to the hell region that interpenetrates above bars and drug dens. These astral plane spirits attach themselves to an embodied person who is drinking or using drugs and vicariously feed off of the energy of that person's use, encouraging them to use more and more. Once out of their physical body, the astral plane spirit can mentally create alcohol or drugs but they can get no relief since they have no physical body; but they can find relief by joining a person who is practicing their addition of choice, whether it is to gain power over others, drugs, alcohol or sex.

PURGATORY

Purgatory attracts those who were truly evil on Earth, those who were brutal, heinous and malevolent. They lived to gain power over others.

In the planes of purgatory, the planes of "middle darkness", billions of Earth's teeming masses congregate. These masses were misled and mistaught on Earth. There is a considerable difference between being basically evil and being the victim of ignorance.

Purgatory is the temporary home of five principal types:

Those who have been misled through unsound religious ideas and must linger until they accept enlightenment.

Those who must linger until some habit acquired on Earth has been overcome.

Some of those who were deranged on Earth, morons, idiots, the truly insane. (Many inhabiting asylums are not insane.)

Atheists and supposed intellectuals who, though they rejected any concept of a Supreme Being, nevertheless were not evil.

Those who became so attached to their Earth life, the wealth, social standing, "things" of Earth, they are Earth bound through their desires, though they are not evil.

Purgatory occupies Borderland, although all in Borderland by no means are in purgatory. Purgatory holds the vast army of souls who while on Earth blocked the potential or desire to seek the light; those who sought no spiritual aim or purpose. Performing no particular evil, neither did they perform anything particularly worthwhile. They simply breathed, ate, slept, worked, existed, drifting socially, morally and spiritually.

Arriving on the other side, they migrate to that stagnant level lying between two active streams of life, the hells and the Highlands. There many are content to continue their stagnation. It is often difficult to "stir up the gift of God" within these drifters. They are content to drift lazily through the days and years.

Many realize they forged the ties that bind them to this mid-plane from which they can extricate themselves. These usually understand early that they took substance released by God and, by their own thoughtlessness, wove it into a state of purgatory for themselves.

Many learn there are dismal depths below and Highlands of light above. They realize that the vast spheres of love and light await their ultimate arrival. Recognizing the cause of their detention, they strive valiantly to gain the Highlands.

Others viciously rebel. They miss everything they possessed on Earth and yearn for return to Earth. Many realizing what a struggle lies ahead to attain even a small measure of what they had on Earth, forfeit any phase of higher plane life and strive to reincarnate at the first opportunity. They witness those who served them as servants or workers inhabiting beautiful homes in heaven, while they languished in a hut on a barren plane. Often a rapid return to Earth is not permitted, it being a "reward" not yet earned. Missionaries from higher planes descend to work among those misguided ones, back to the path of Divine Order. Ascension from one plane to a higher plane must be earned.

Purgatory also is found to be almost an exact counterpart of certain areas of the physical world, not the place of beauty, but the barren spots, or the overcrowded ghettos. Arrivals in purgatory quickly realize that dropping the earthly physical body simply strips them of all externals and leaves the moral character unchanged, that the sins of the inner Human are deeper that the epidermis, that death does not transform an ugly character into a beautiful personality any more than walking through a college can make a philosopher of a fool. One comes face to face with their true self.

Often self-created memories bring remorse, and due restitution must be made for errors. But every kind word spoken, every generous deed committed, every sympathy expressed, every truth vindicated, every pure principle upheld, helps to lift the soul toward the Highlands.

Every atom in our aura is impressed with good or ill, retaining the impress until the slate is wiped clean by the one who wrote the record. The very air around us is an errorless archive, an unwinding scroll, on pages are forever written all that one does, thinks, or says. Over there are inscribed the records of our inner lives.

Purgatory, not hell, is now the repository for the hordes of souls departing Earth. Most are not evil souls, but countless thousands of lives are ruined by drugs, alcohol or loose morals. These are only misguided victims of misjudgment.

Once Humans learn they will go on living life eternally, they will come to know that they can only live it properly by loving it. Humans must stop smiling in condescension at the idea of life after death, and begin working in harmony with the laws which prevail between the two Worlds. Once it is established that there is another world lying all about them, that it has dangers as well as its beauties and blessings, only then can this World begin to become the light it was meant to be in God's universe. Learning what life is like over there can make life more meaningful here.

Every soul on Earth, regardless of nation, should make it their business to spread the truth of life after death, to teach others to prepare themselves for the afterlife; to teach those still on the Earth the importance of overcoming their negative desires, negative habits and addictions.

The penalty of sin always falls upon the one most responsible. Justice demands that those who suffer unjustly at the hands of others must be compensated for their suffering, while those causing the suffering must themselves suffer. Mercy abounds on the Earth plane, while justice prevails on the astral.

THE HIGHLAND

There are no hard lines of demarcation between the ascending planes of Etheria. It is only that the grayness gradually becomes less dense and the landscapes, homes, clothing, seem to emit a brighter hue. Entire surroundings become increasingly beautiful and heavenly fragrance permeates each ascending plane.

Highland cities are made from material more malleable than Earth substances so they lose their appearance of solidity. This material responds to the Law of Higher Frequency. The buildings become mansions surrounded by indescribably beautiful grounds.

The ascending planes are a spiritual universe of unimaginable immensity and grandeur, with sphere upon sphere of the realms of light stretching away to infinity. Each ascending sphere expresses the light brighter, the inhabitants are more calm and serene, more illuminated, until one attains a point beyond which one can see.

On the further side lie the angelic regions. The atmosphere is permeated with a light of such brilliance a Human cannot yet endure it. Our minds cannot as yet fully comprehend the glory of that which is pure spirit. Life in the Highlands is an active life, a social life, a constructive life, a retributive life, a progressive life; the Otherworld is a sphere of spiritual growth and moral conquest. Whereas on Earth the attitude is to attain material success, in Etheria each striving is for progression of the soul, gained only by aspiration, persistent altruistic effort and unselfish endeavor.

The light of the astral plane is not the light of our physical sun. Everything that exists, from comet to stone, gives off an auric essence. Therefore every astral form emanates a light, according to its spiritual advancement. A flow of cosmic radiance emanates from the higher planes and pervades the astral ethers with a cosmic light just as our sun illuminates Earth.

Earth and Earth life is a workshop, a schoolroom, a training ground for life on higher planes. On Earth the Human form must be fed, clothed and housed. In the afterlife the soul meets the challenge of molding matter to conform to the spirit's needs.

19.
Methods of Contacting the Spirit World

AUTOMATIC WRITING

There are many different ways to contact the Spirit World or for us to contact our soul. One of the methods some beginners are tempted to use is automatic writing, which I do not suggest to you, but will cover it here just for information's sake.

First of all, using automatic writing or an Ojai board will most likely connect a person only the astral spirits and often time mischievous spirits. Ojai boards are sold in the game section of stores. Communicating with the Spirit World should not be attempted as a game because one can get connected to a spirit or a group of astral spirits that can block a person from being in communication with their own soul. No matter what method you choose to use to attempt Spirit communication, it is highly recommended that you ask only to communicate with levels of your own Oversoul.

Automatic writing is not recommended for the same reason; you are most likely going to attract an astral plane spirit that is not serious or advanced and what they give you can be misleading and/or confusing. To produce automatic writing, the entity or entities control the writer's hand. An energetic tie must be created between the two minds. Once the astral spirit impresses ideas they wish to write upon the writer's brain, they simultaneously induce the physical hand to trace out the words on paper. This influence is affected through magnetism.

Pencil, paper, and solitude are necessary if one attempts automatic writing. The person seeking connection should seal the room they are in on the North, South, East and West, the ceiling and the floor from any negative or astral entities and say a prayer before they begin. It is not necessary to enter a trance to make this kind of connection. The purpose of a pencil rather than a ball point pen is that a wooden pencil and the lead in a pencil are better conductors of magnetic energy than a pen. The words from the spirit send thoughts to the writer and the writer receives the thoughts as they flow into their consciousness. The hand is the vehicle which translates the thoughts into a flow of words. The spirit "throws" the thought into the mind of the automatist, at the same time projecting a flow of magnetism into the radial nerve in the arm and hand so that words are written through the flow of electric impulses.

The spirit never impresses the brain of the automatist directly. Rather it impresses the mind substance which, through the electric threads, sends the communication into the brain of the automatist. The brain is the transformer. The actual spelling of the words must be drawn from the automatist's conscious memory and vocabulary. The quality of the information depends on the education and vocabulary of both the spirit and the writer.

The greatest handicap of the spirits is finding proper language to express their thoughts. Often there are no Earth words that can bring their ideas into written form. The laws of the two worlds differ, and it is most difficult to describe the Laws of the Spirit World in Earth's language. Often the communication must happen at the level of symbols, pictures or images rather than words.

One should use great caution in giving their consciousness over to an unseen being even to a being at the Master level. It is highly recommended that spiritual communication happen through telepathy rather than through automatic writing. No communication should be accepted and followed blindly just because it was received from the other side whether the information comes in automatic writing or any other form of Spirit communication.

Rules to follow when attempting automatic writing:
1. Sit only at a specific time decided upon previously with yourself and the Spirits.
2. Plan for no more than ten minutes to half an hour daily in the beginning.
3. Sit at the same location, which becomes magnetized.
4. Always keep the mind prayerful, earnest and sincere.
5. Should the communication become frivolous or ludicrous, stop immediately. Psychic centers can be prematurely opened, voices

heard which cannot be controlled and such occurrences are extremely difficult to correct and can possibly lead to emotional and mental instability.
6. Demand to connect only with higher plane Spirits.
7. Parents should never allow an Ouija board into their home, because children are susceptible to attracting mischievous spirits.
8. Do not avoid spiritual communication simply because of the risks. To do so is to give your power to those who try to deliberately side tract your spiritual enfoldment. Keep your consciousness in the Light of Love and remember to go by the rules.

PLEDGE FEVER

It is important that once we have committed and pledged ourselves to our spiritual path that we maintain balance in our lives. It is easy, especially once spiritual contact is made, to focus on having spiritual communication and ignore or avoid doing the physical and emotional things that keep us balanced.

If one turns fanatically to develop any phase of ESP, giving too much thought and effort or through the use of drugs aimed toward the goal of swift enfoldment, that person may fall victim to hallucinations. It is always wise to spend only an hour a day in psychic unfoldment practices and not overdo your efforts.

Anyone who attempts any kind of psychic unfoldment would do well to keep their mind grounded through mundane occupations requiring a great deal of attention. As one pursues meditation and spiritual practices, sharpened intuition will be the first indication of approaching clairaudience.

CLAIRAUDIENCE

Clairaudience is receiving spiritual information as a sound or a voice. It is necessary to make necessary inner changes to be available to hear Spirits.
1. Mental attitude
2. Expectancy
3. Practice of exercises that influence our perception of sound vibrations other than those we ordinarily hear
4. Relaxation, concentration and focus.

Being able to hear spiritually is available within the vibration of the Third, Fourth and the lowest Fifth dimensions. Being able to see spiritually is possible within the Third and Fourth vibration. It is important to remember that many of us came into these incarnations from higher planes where all is silent and everything occurs telepathically. Because of this, it is really beneficial to tell our soul we are willing to receive information as knowingness rather than demanding to hear or see spiritually.

Clairaudience, like clairvoyance, is a higher sense than the five physical senses. In order to experience it, we must suspend our conscious connection with the physical so that we may become attuned to the higher sense or vibration.

First attempts at meditations for the specific purpose of developing clairaudience may bring few results during the actual periods of meditation. However, after concentrated effort, one may find that while reading a book, for example, they will hear the sound of a voice faintly, so dim and distant that it is indistinguishable. When reading, one fulfills the necessary requirements of both relaxation and concentration enabling the voice from another vibratory realm to be heard. The first and most important requisite for having a clairaudient experience is the ability to relax and concentrate one-pointedly upon one object.

There are two main aspects or divisions of clairaudient faculty; *objective* and *subjective*. Objective clairaudience is the perception of a sound that seems to be heard in the same manner as normal sound. It's "point of origin" is outside the individual, as if someone were speaking at a distance of from one to three feet from the hearer. Any other person who had developed the faculty of clairaudience would also hear it.

Subjective clairaudience is the perception of a sound, which has its point of expression directly upon the auditory nerve system of the hearer. It is "heard" inside one's head and cannot be "heard" by another person, however clairaudient they may be.

In objective clairaudience, sounds seem to fall upon the ear as do normal sounds. In subjective clairaudience, sounds are heard inwardly as though the ear mechanism were bypassed. Sound as we basically understand it is not necessary to clairaudience. In ordinary hearing, sound waves enter the ear and through the ear mechanisms of membranes, fluids, air space and tiny bones, finally strike and stimulate the auditory nerve. Every sound we hear quickly becomes a thought or idea in our mind. It is no longer purely sound vibration as it becomes a mind vibration.

Persons in Etheria can mentally direct to the auditory nerve itself a type of sound vibration which is not usually caught by the ear mechanism and this vibration traveling along the auditory nerve is then transmitted directly to the seat of thought. The sound is such that it is not caught by the physical ear, but is transmitted by the auditory nerve itself.

As the vibration passes through this nerve it is recorded in the brain as sound, just as when Earth sound impulses enter the ear. It would have sound, but would be heard only by the one to whom it is directed. This is subjective clairaudience, because the manifestation point of receptivity is the auditory nerve of the hearer.

This is the type of clairaudience most commonly experience. Most people do not realize that the point of sound origin is just inside the ear, not outside. It seems to them as if the sound is directly at the ear, when in most cases it is actually striking the auditory nerve.

The sound vibration could also be pointed directly to the seat of thought, bypassing the auditory nerve entirely. If this is done, the sense of sound or the feel of sound would happen, but there would be no actual hearing of the sound itself. This is also a type of subjective clairaudience.

Everything in existence, both animate and inanimate, you and I, a piece of rock, a delicate flower, is constantly emitting a sound or combination of sounds. This planet, this solar system, this Universe, each emits a certain sound or tone combination, which is projected into and permeates the ethers.

The ancient Hindu sages believed that God created the Universe though the sound of OM. Thus when an individual properly chants or speaks OM they are reflecting, and attuning themselves, to Universal Sound.

In our heads there exists a remarkable Human radio, a receiving set for tuning into Universal Intelligence. It is not necessary to understand how the mechanism of the pituitary and the pineal glands actually work. It is sufficient to know that, just as God provided faculties for our outer hearing, so have we been provided an inner mechanism capable of registering sounds above the terrestrial.

**Always keep yourself surrounded
with the Pure White Light of the Christ.**

DEVELOPMENT OF CLAIRVOYANCE

Here is a suggested exercise for developing clairvoyance, thought transference or telepathy. Have a friend assist you with this exercise who will be in another part of the house. You need several articles to perform this exercise:

1. A small, blue, ten watt electric light bulb;
2. A mirror;
3. Orange construction paper;
4. A deck of cards, preferably Tarot (The cards are optional);
5. A package of double-faced adhesive tape.

From the orange paper, cut a disk the size of a quarter, tape it and place it upon your forehead, between the eyes, at the root of your nose.

Sit in a darkened room, lighted only with the blue light. Sit approximately one to two feet from the mirror. Fasten your concentrated attention upon the orange disk in the mirror's reflection. Hold it there for five minutes. At the end of that time turn off the blue light, close your eyes, and wait to see if you can receive the vision being projected by a fellow experimenter who is mentally sending you the picture of a certain card upon which they are concentrating intently as you begin your receptivity at the moment you extinguish the blue light.

If you are practicing telepathy with a partner you may wish to use Tarot cards or ordinary playing cards or just random objects your friend may hold for you to focus upon.

During the first week of practice, gaze at the disk for only three minutes. The second week increase it to five minutes and add two more minutes each week until you attain a fifteen-minute period of concentrated attention upon the disk. Try not to blink your eyes. If tears come, let them. If you find your mind wandering:

1. Concentrate on your slow breathing, inhaling and exhaling, or
2. Concentrate on the word OM, mentally as you inhale and exhale.

In either case, do not let the mind wander from the orange disk.

If you prefer to practice alone rather than with a partner, you will be striving for clairvoyance rather than telepathy.

When you are practicing alone or with a partner, for clairvoyance or for telepathy, you may experience various sensations. The disk may appear black, or disappear completely. In fact, your entire figure may disappear, and you see strange things around you or the room may appear to be filled with mist. Another face may seem to transfigure your own. You may feel a sensation of spiraling upward mentally. Do not become alarmed at anything you may see or feel. Keep gazing steadily.

Whether you practice with a partner or not, you will be developing the faculty of clairvoyance or the ability of telepathy the act of projecting your thoughts or receiving thoughts from other people on Earth or beings from other dimensions.

TYPES OF TRANCE

A trance is defined as a disconnection of the physical senses from the conscious awareness and direction. One of the difficulties in defining trance is that there are several distinct types of trance, each of which would require an entirely different definition. The types are:

1. Conscious trance
2. Semi-conscious trance
3. Deep or cataleptic trance
4. Yogic trance
5. Samadhi
6. Trance through hypnosis

CONSCIOUS TRANCE

In *conscious trance* the physical faculties are not disconnected from one's awareness, but are disconnected from their direction. Sometimes we might walk or drive and go into a meditative state and find ourselves blocks or even miles past where we were going. That is a light conscious trance when the consciousness is operating at the moment in the mental body and not in the physical.

The same thing can happen when we are reading a book and suddenly realize we've been thinking of something else and have been reading the same line over and over, unaware of its content. That is also a light conscious trance.

A SEMI-CONSCIOUS TRANCE

In a *semi-conscious trance*, it is possible to experience a state of consciousness in which one seemingly floats back and forth between the physical World and the higher Worlds, without actually leaving the physical body as in a deep trance. It could be likened to the state of consciousness experience when one is half awake and half asleep, mentally drifting. This is an excellent time to see psychic visions, or hear music or voices and to retain the memory of them.

It is during this half-awake sleep period that the mind learns best and retains the learning in memory. The mind does not learn or retain as well while in a state of deep sleep. It learns and retains better during the early morning hours when one is refreshed by several hours of deep sleep and their mind is reposing in a lighter state of consciousness.

This "drifting" state of consciousness is attained often while we are meditating and it is called the alpha state of brain frequency and is an excellent state to cultivate. Try to bring your mind to that completely relaxed condition, but hold alert attention of mind so that you do not lose consciousness and fall into the delta state of brain frequency as you do when you fall asleep.

CATALEPTIC TRANCE

Cataleptic trance renders the body rigid and apparently lifeless. In fact, physicians have pronounced a patient dead, only to discover they were in a cataleptic trance. In these instances it is unusual for the consciousness to recall anything which occurred during its absence from the body.

A *coma* is a different situation. Often the person in a coma while their physical bodies are in the coma state they are vividly awake on the astral and striving to make people around them aware that they can hear but not speak.

Cataleptic usually is brought about through accident rather than by desire on the part of the individual; a direct result of a nervous disorder or illness, rather than a trained mental effort. The body is, in all appearances, quite lifeless and there is no evidence of pulse or heartbeat during catalepsy.

However, the silver cord between the Spirit and the body remains intact, and therein lays the difference between death and catalepsy, even though the consciousness may retain no remembrance of having been on the astral. One in a cataleptic trance will sooner or later awaken as life force returns to the physical form. The heartbeat begins once again and the pulse becomes detectable. Cataleptic trace remains a mystery to doctors and scientists.

YOGIC TRANCE

There are two types of *yogic trance*. In one, the individual leaves his body, retaining full consciousness on the astral and a memory of all that occurs while they are out of their body. In the other, a person remains in the body, but experiences a state of superior or expanded consciousness. The body is not asleep. The only obvious change is in the consciousness.

One may be aware of any number of spiritual experiences while in the yogic trance; clairvoyance, clairaudience, astral projection, or telepathy. The person may be out of their body but the body remains normal, as in a state of sleep. One can experience some of these phases while their body is simply relaxed and not asleep.

In a yogic trance, the consciousness is lifted into a state that enables the individual to glimpse another World and hear voices from another World, yet they still will be conscious on the physical plane and remain in their body.

SAMADHI

One who has mastered the ability to leave their physical body in a state of trance and travel in higher realms, both in consciousness and in space, has attained one of the highest states of consciousness possible while dwelling in the mortal body. Such a state is called *Samadhi*, a Sanskrit word from India. Samadhi is the ultimate attainment of anyone who has spent years, perhaps lives, in deep mental concentration upon God, and has kept within their soul a never-ceasing, all consuming desire to know God.

If you will seek to unite with the Oversoul, and spend your time in concentration upon this particular attainment, your attained psychic faculties will be on a much higher scale; this not to say that one should discontinue the practice of unfolding clairaudience, astral projection, and other spiritual gifts. But we are to keep ever in our mind that these psychic phases should be aligned with a great unfoldment of the High Self which is over lighting us.

TRANCE THROUGH HYPNOSIS

Hypnotism can be a marvelous process in the hands of the adept hypnotist, or it can be extremely dangerous in the hands of one not trained in occultism, and who deals in the art simply for sensationalism or in ignorance.

SELF-INDUCED TRANCE

Entering a trance state is not always pleasant in the beginning because in a sense it is a type of "death." It is a separation of the consciousness from the physical vehicle. Most people, even though they sincerely desire to experience trance, simply do not know how to let go of their physical senses to the point of entering that mental state. It is difficult at first, but as one become practiced it becomes easier.

Different people will experience different sensations while going into the trance state. Some people experience a feeling similar to descending in a fast elevator. Some people experience a rapid ascent with a spiraling sensation and their body even moves in a circular movement. Some people experience a feeling of falling; some others experience a sensation of contracting within themselves as if their physical body remains its normal size, but they have a feeling of shrinking within their physical shell.

These are the most common sensations: falling, rising, and contraction, none of which sound pleasant, but they pass as one becomes adept at entering the trance state.

It is possible to enter a self-induced trance state by imagining yourself standing before some huge purple curtains or drapes. You mentally imagine parting the drapes in the center and stepping through and beyond them, with the feeling that you are leaving your physical body on one side while you are stepping through to the other side; by using every ounce of your mental energy to do so you are developing an excellent means of projecting your astral body.

When I first began to meditate in the early 80's, I was able to put myself into a trance state with very little effort. At that time, I would do it so that a higher vibrational level of my Oversoul could speak and teach through my body. I would deliberately leave my body and Matthew, a level of my higher self or one of the Ascended Masters, would take over the body and speak. His voice was very different than mine and his accent sounded Irish or maybe Tibetan. When it was one of the Masters, the voice was much stronger and powerful than my voice and often strained my vocal chords. People very much enjoyed the wisdom brought through and were impressed with the change in my voice and features. I perceived myself to be near the ceiling observing what was happening, but disconnected from the thoughts he was bringing through. After each session I would find that I felt very tired since our vibrations were so different at that time.

After a couple of years of doing sessions for people by going into a trance, my soul convinced me that Matthew and I could do the sessions telepathically rather than him taking over my body. At first I felt insecure taking on the responsibility of repeating what he gave me in my own voice. The audience preferred the proof that the information was coming from a higher source indicated by the change in my voice and many people who were used to receiving his teaching and guidance through me dropped out of my life. Since I was the one receiving and transmitting the information, I knew the source was the same. It took a while for my ego and confidence to adjust to the change.

The Spiritual Hierarchy no longer recommends that we give our bodies over to another entity to speak through us, but they do recommend allowing higher level entities to teach through our vehicles through the use of telepathy, I find this to be much easier on my body and brain than allowing the merging to happen.

USING A CRYSTAL BALL

Concentrate first upon taking slow, deep breaths, focusing your attention upon the ball. Breathe until you have developed a steady level of concentration. If your mind wanders, draw it back. Force it to concentrate only upon the ball, and look easily, but one-pointedly, into it. Do not stare. Relax the eyes and blink naturally. Do not look into the ball, but look through it. Try to imagine it as being a doorway into another World and gaze steadily through the doorway.

During these meditations different things may happen. The entire crystal ball may disappear from your sight. This will not mean that it has actually dematerialized; it will mean that your Inner Eye is beginning to come into focus, or that your consciousness is beginning to expand.

Another possibility is that the ball may appear to suddenly cloud over. This will occur more frequently in connection with clairvoyance than with entering the trance state. In another instance it may seem as if you are gliding effortlessly toward the ball and finding yourself suddenly standing on the threshold of another World. The ball will indeed become a doorway into another vibrational realm.

It may require many periods of meditation to accomplish this, but remember that each time you meditate you draw nearer to these experiences. Your powers of concentration become more acute, and these heightened mental powers will result in increased material success in your everyday life. It will enhance your mental alertness, your ability to make sudden and correct decisions, and to unfold your intuitive powers.

Another exercise requires the use of a lighted candle. This may be placed before a mirror into which you gaze either into the light of the reflected candle or at your own reflection. You may gaze into the flame itself. It is easier if the room is darkened.

As you enter your period of concentration, let your breathing be slow and deep. However, if giving attention to breathing tends to distract your mind from concentrating upon the focal point, forget monitoring your breath and just focus your attention upon the flame. All these exercises should be practiced in a quiet room. Some people feel they find it easier to concentrate at midnight or in the early hours of the morning when much of the electrical interference around them has ceased.

I give you these suggestions from my own experiences and I accept no responsibility for how you use them.

www.ingramcontent.com/pod-product-compliance
Lightning Source LLC
Chambersburg PA
CBHW020357170426
43200CB00005B/202